I0142383

The
Year
of the
Poet VI

July 2019

The Poetry Posse

inner child press, ltd.

The Poetry Posse 2019

Gail Weston Shazor

Shareef Abdur Rasheed

Teresa E. Gallion

hülya n. yılmaz

Kimberly Burnham

Tzemin Ition Tsai

Elizabeth Esguerra Castillo

Jackie Davis Allen

Joe Paire

Caroline 'Ceri' Nazareno

Ashok K. Bhargava

Alicja Maria Kuberska

Swapna Behera

Albert 'Infinite' Carrasco

Eliza Segiet

William S. Peters, Sr.

General Information

The Year of the Poet VI
July 2019 Edition

The Poetry Posse

1st Edition : 2019

Publisher Information

1st Edition : Inner Child Press
intouch@innerchildpress.com
www.innerchildpress.com

$ 12.99

WHAT WOULD LIFE BE WITHOUT A LITTLE POETRY?

Dedication

This Book is dedicated to

Poetry . . .

The Poetry Posse

past, present & future

our Patrons and Readers

the Spirit of our Everlasting Muse

&

the Power of the Pen

to effectuate change!

In the darkness of my life
I heard the music
I danced . . .
and the Light appeared
and I dance

Janet P. Caldwell

Table of Contents

The Poetry Posse

Table of Contents . . . *continued*

July Featured Poets   115

Inner Child News   145

Other Anthological Works   167

Foreword

Only a single bird
is singing
The air is cloning it.
We hear through mirrors.

Federico Garcia Lorca

This month's theme is Africa and Horn Africa.

Africa and Horn Africa are the mirrors of singing birds, flora and fauna, cultural prominence, collective life, social translators of ethnic groups those who grow with the nature. The inhabitants are the crisis manager of all adversities and the echo of their brave History .

Africa is a continent   but Horn Africa is a peninsula in Northeast Africa. It extends hundreds of kilometres into the Arabian sea and lies along the Southern side of the Gulf of Eden .The area   is the easternmost projection of the African Continent. The countries and territories included are Djibouti, Eritrea, Ethiopia and Somalia. The people of the Horn Africa are subdivided into six people clusters; Beja, Cushitic, Ethio-Semitic, Omotic, Oromo and Somalia. Somalia is a country located in the Horn of Africa bordered by Ethiopia to the West, Djibouti to the northwest, the Gulf of Aden to the North, the

ix

Somali Sea, Guardafui Channel to the east and Kenya to the South East.

The Horn Africa enjoys an excellent strategic location south west of the Red Sea and Gulf of Aden. Its location on one side of some of the world's major trade lanes and land route gives it vital importance because of its proximity to the oil reach Arabian Peninsula. Part of the Horn Africa is also known as the Somali Peninsula.

Mostly mountainous, the region arose through faults resulting from the rift valley. Agriculture is the single most important activity in Africa. We cannot overlook the tradition, the nativism, the culture and the contribution of Africa and horn Africa for the generations. Nativism is a celebration of the pluralism that is the very core tune of Africa and Horn Africa.

Somalia is known to the Egyptians as the Land of Punt. Punt was famous for frankincense and myrrh. Around 100 Somali Diaspora communities exist across the West, which actively are engaged in thousands of Civil associations. Lake Assal is a saline lake below sea level making it the lowest point on the land of the Horn of Africa. Some farming knowledge passed down from generation to generation has become obsolete. Drought crippled the region. People struggle to recover from the natural calamity.

Inner Child Press International® with its mission of *building bridges of cultural understanding* takes the responsibility for global peace and harmony through poetry with International festivals and Anthologies. We respect the land, nature, folk tales, culture, music, literature, perceptions, ideas, thoughts, language and all ethnic groups of the world.

Poetry is the living nature and nature is the living poetry.

We respect the humanity   ...
We respect the survival skills.
We respect the indigenous knowledge.
Let us join our hands for peace ....

Swapna Behera
Cultural Ambassador of India and south East Asia for Inner Child Press International

Preface

Dear Family and Friends,

Yes I am excited? This year we have aligned our vision with that of UNESCO as it honors and acknowledges a variety of Global Indigenous cultures. We are now in our sixth year of publication. As are on our way to hitting another milestone. Needless to say, I am elated. Our initial vision was to just perform at this level for the year of 2014. Since that time we have had the blessed opportunity to include many other wonderful word artists and storytellers in the Poetry Posse from lands, cultures and persuasions all over the world. We have featured hundreds of additional poets, thereby introducing their poetic offerings to our vast global readership.

In keeping with our effort and vision to expand the awareness of poets from all walks by making this offerings accessible, we at Inner Child Press International will continue to make every volume a FREE Download. The books are also available for purchase at the affordable cost of $7.00 per volume.

In the previous years, our monthly themes were Flowers, Birds, Gemstones, Trees and Past Cultures. This year we have elected to continue the

Cultural theme. In each month's volume you will have the opportunity to not only read at least one poem themed by our Poetry Posse members about such culture, but we have included a few words about the culture in our prologue. The reasoning behind this is that now our poetry has the opportunity to be educational for not only the reader, but we poets as well. We hope you find the poetic offerings insightful as we use our poetic form to relay to you what we too have learned through our research in making our offering available to you, our readership.

In closing, we would like to thank you for being an integral part of our amazing journey.

Enjoy our amazing featured poets . . . they are amazing!

Building Cultural Bridges of Understanding . . .

Bless Up . . . From the home in our hearts to yours

Bill

The Poetry Posse
Inner Child Press Ineternational

PS

Do Not forget about the World Healing, World Peace Poetry effort.

Available here

www.worldhealingworldpeacepoetry.com

**For Free Downloads of Previous Issues of
The Year of the Poet**

www.innerchildpress.com/the-year-of-the-poet

poetry is . . . .

India INK

The Horn of Africa

The "Horn of Africa" is of the most eastern part of the Mother Land'. It extends sever thousand kilometers into the Arabian Sea.

Traditionally "The Horn of Africa" included solely the countries of Djibouti, Eritrea, Ethiopia and Somalia. The cultures of these countries have been linked together in similarity and congruity for many centuries and continue to this day. Of late other countries such as Kenya, Sudan, South Sudan and Uganda have been included in the demographic description. The 'Horn of Africa has also been called the "Somalian Peninsula" which primarily refers to Somalia and Easter Ethiopia.

For more information about the culture and people of this region, visit :

https://en.wikipedia.org/wiki/Horn_of_Africa

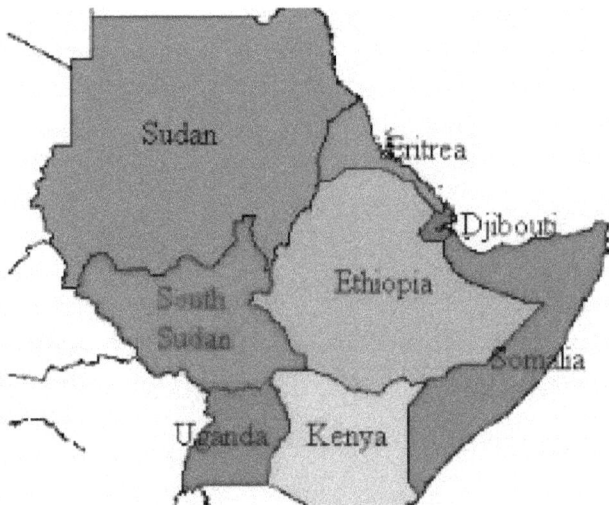

Poets . . .
sowing seeds in the
Conscious Garden of Life,
that those who have yet to come
may enjoy the Flowers.

Poets, Writers . . . know that we are the enchanting magicians that nourishes the seeds of dreams and thoughts . . . it is our words that entice the hearts and minds of others to believe there is something grand about the possibilities that life has to offer and our words tease it forth into action . . . for you are the Poet, the Writer to whom the Gift of Words has been entrusted . . .

~ wsp

I Fly

because I Can

... said the Dreamer to the world.

www.iamjustbill.com

Coming
April 2020

Inner Child Press International

The
World Healing, World Peace
International Poetry Symposium

Stay Tuned

for more information

intouch@innerchildpress.com

'building bridges of cultural understanding'

www.innerchildpress.com

Poetry succeeds where instruction fails.

~ wsp

Gail Weston Shazor

This is a creative promise ~ my pen will speak to and for the world. Enamored with letters and respectful of their power, I have been writing for most of my life. A mother, daughter, sister and grandmother I give what I have been given, greatfilledly.

Author of . . .

"An Overstanding of an Imperfect Love"
&
Notes from the Blue Roof

Lies My Grandfathers Told Me

available at Inner Child Press.

www.facebook.com/gailwestonshazor
www.innerchildpress.com/gail-weston-shazor
navypoet1@gmail.com

The Holy Mother
Haiku

The Holy Mother's

Horn protrudes into the world

See her influence

Poetry

I pen from a well of need
That you may know me
My heart, thoughts and desires
My observations on the state of
My perpetual disarray
The words and phrases infinite
In combination, like yours and different
One and the same

The taste of a poet's tongue
Is ever sweet, sharp, bitter
Will make you think and feel
And sometimes, just sometimes
Look inside yourself
Yet always truthful when
Laid out for you to examine
A flavor ripened in the universe
From which we pull the power
To share the essentialness of life

Lovers? You and I are always
Whether touching ink to ink
Or inspiring me to feel you
Your words cause goosebumps
To form along the nerves of my spine
Your heart on paper is a holy thing
And I weep in your beauty
I laugh in your joy
I cry in your poignancy
Your limitlessness sets my soul free
To return to your pen again and again

Letter to My Future Love

I am here waiting on you
My heart is in need of healing
I have used this fence to hold it together
But it only holds the pieces
In the hollow of my chest
I don't understand how my love
Could have destroyed me
And yet I yearn for your touch

I am here waiting on you
To help me heal myself
So that when I gift it to you
It is perfect again
Free of the mistakes I have made
Free of the choices I have made

I am here waiting on you
Looking for those rare moments
When we laugh at the same thing
When you can complete my word
Before I even know that there is more
That hasn't been said

I am here waiting on you
To hold my hand in the grocery
In between the oranges and ice cream
To eat the popcorn out my bag
At the movies
And wrap your jacket around me
Until I get to the car

I am here waiting on you
To slide the shirt off my shoulder
Just to kiss my collarbone
To wrap your arms around me
While I wash and you wait to dry
To call me in from cooking
To share a silly commercial

I am here waiting in you
To allow me to wrap my legs around you
And pull you close to me
To be ready with desire
Hungry for the feel of you
To taste every inch of your skin
On the tip of my tongue

I am here waiting for you
To prove that love is strong
And faithful and true
To show me what it's like
To know you unconditionally
In good times and trying times
I want to know that wherever we are
That our love will remain special
So until then
I am here waiting on you

Gail Weston Shazor

Alicja Maria Kuberska

Alicja Maria Kuberska – awarded Polish poetess, novelist, journalist, editor. She was born in 1960, in Świebodzin, Poland. She now lives in Inowrocław, Poland.

In 2011 she published her first volume of poems entitled: "The Glass Reality". Her second volume "Analysis of Feelings", was published in 2012. The third collection "Moments" was published in English in 2014, both in Poland and in the USA. In 2014, she also published the novel - "Virtual roses" and volume of poems "On the border of dream". Next year her volume entitled "Girl in the Mirror" was published in the UK and "Love me" , " (Not)my poem" in the USA. In 2015 she also edited anthology entitled "The Other Side of the Screen".

In 2016 she edited two volumes: "Taste of Love" (USA), "Thief of Dreams" (Poland) and international anthology entitled " Love is like Air" (USA). In 2017 she published volume entitled "View from the window" (Poland). She also edits series of anthologies entitled "Metaphor of Contemporary" (Poland)

Her poems have been published in numerous anthologies and magazines in Poland, the USA, the UK, Albania, Belgium, Chile, Spain, Israel, Canada, India, Italy, Uzbekistan, Czech Republic, South Korea and Australia. She was a featured poet of New Mirage Journal (USA) in the summer of 2011.

Alicja Kuberska is a member of the Polish Writers Associations in Warsaw, Poland and IWA Bogdani, Albania. She is also a member of directors' board of Soflay Literature Foundation.

Lake Victoria

It was once called a huge stain of water
and it spilled on the hot and thirsty African soil.

Man turned the basin into a meadow.
Green plants covered the blue water.

Nature entangled water hyacinths in a mourning wreath.
It threw a thick shroud on the shiny surface of water.

The greed and stupidity of humans broke the ecosystem to
shreds.
It is delicate and complicated like the spider's web.

Now the fish – invaders live In the depths of the lake.
Old species died - they lost the fight with intruders.

The cradle of the Nile turned into a graveyard.
Plankton disappeared and life-giving oxygen, too.

The rainbow

I look for the rainbow every day.
It does not matter that the day is
Gloomy, foggy, cheerless
And the sky is covered by
Heavy, stormy clouds.

The rainbow sleeps
In the drops of rain.
Warmed with sunshine,
It stretches on the sky like a bow
And blooms with six colors.

I blow away the worries
Together with grey fog

Little town

I walk along the streets of the town,
Which I once loved.
Today, I am an indifferent stranger.
I barely recognize it.

There are no more old, hospitable aunts.
No more nosy neighbors hidden behind curtains,
Or brave men with war stories.
They are gone.

Time changed everything,
Not only the people, houses, streets and trees.
It seems to me that it even
Repainted the shade of the sky.

Jackie
Davis
Allen

Jackie Davis Allen

Jackie Davis Allen, otherwise known as Jacqueline D. Allen or Jackie Allen, grew up in the Cumberland Mountains of Appalachia. As the next eldest daughter of a coal miner father and a stay at home mother, she was the first in her family to attend and graduate from college. Her siblings, in their own right, are accomplished, though she is the only one, to date, that has discovered the gift of writing.

Graduating from Radford University, with a Bachelors of Science degree in Early Education, she taught in both public and private schools. For over a decade she taught private art classes to children both in her home and at a local Art and Framing Shop where she also sold her original soft sculptured Victorian dolls and original christening gowns.

She resides in northern Virginia with her husband, taking much needed get-aways to their mountain home near the Blue Ridge Mountains, a place that evokes memories of days spent growing up in the Appalachian Mountains.

A lover of hats, she has worn many. Following marriage to her college sweetheart, and as wife, mother, grandmother, teacher, tutor, artist, writer, poet and crafter, she is a lover of art and antiques, surrounding herself, always, with books, seeking to learn more.

In 2015 she authored *Looking for Rainbows, Poetry, Prose and Art*, and in 2017, *Dark Side of the Moon*. Both books of mostly narrative poetry were published by Inner Child Press and were edited by hulya n. yilmaz.

http://www.innerchildpress.com/jackie-davis-allen.php
jackiedavisallen.com

A Snapshot

The Horn of Africa is a peninsula
in Northeast Africa consisting of four countries:
Ethiopia, Djibouti, Somalia, and Eritrea.

More than 700 square miles, 100+ million people.

Some ancient inhabitants were writers, painters,
architects, musicians, farmers.
Lovers of education, literature.

How fortunate to have discovered these facts!

Some of their peoples practice traditional religions
while others still practice Christianity,
Judaism and Islam

As they have for many centuries.

On Stage

A major heat wave arrives, strives

To scorch the green of the earth.

Colorful birds, in parch of thirst, flit

And flutter between, beneath the trees.

Congregating, as if I had invited them,

To a party, are a host of cardinals, robins.

Their babies, a family of woodpeckers,

A Canada Jay, and a tiny hummingbird.

They search the grass and the garden

For insects, worms, for anything to eat.

These little ones are so appreciative

For the showering blessing the rains provide,

And that which flows from my landscape's water hose.

In return, with joy, they gift me with their presence.

The Noose that Strangles the Truth

With all the political-correctness-buzzing by Enablers,
On Propaganda's Air Waves, I've considered taking a nap,
Hibernating just long enough to wake up and see a new
Day has arisen, a day when the Nation has chosen again,

A strong Leader, one beholden only to the people.

A leader with strong values,
One that supports the Constitution,
One who loves America and its people
And wants to make America Great Again.

It isn't as easy as that, of course.

One cannot bury one's Head in the sand.
Though many do, caring not for truth, for legality,
Wanting only to avoid being caught
In the quagmire of deceptions. And its Lies.

A Patriot once said, "Give me Liberty or give me Death".

I say, Those Who do not Rise up to Support
And Lift up our country Are the same ones who wish
To Drag it back down into the morass, Back into a land
Where Truth, Ethics and Morality wear blindfolds.

And speak out of both sides of their mouth.

Where citizens lives are discounted, where "all" lives don't
Matter. Where Top Secret, Eyes only, and Confidential
Documents Are handled as if Secrets are to be hung out
To dry. For Anyone to see, to be Snatched off the line.

Never mind that the intent was Overt. (She says not).

Understand this: it did and does make a difference.
So here's your chance to Win the Lottery. Stand up! Kick
the Incompetents out: the rampant, Negligent Nincompoops
that would drag our country into ruin.

The Guilty one says, "What difference Does It Make?"

Some would, by party stance, Dance on the Rights Of our
Citizens, our Heroes, our Military, our Veterans, Our
Police, and the Legal Immigrants. They're the ones Who
Safeguard the Rights endowed to us.

By the Constitution.

We hold these rights most dear.
We will Not be Taxed into Subservience,
Nor Led into the Cult that would further Bankrupt us
And our children's children.

Propaganda is the Noose that Strangles the Truth!

Stand up before it's too late!
Quash the Party Line that would make of our country
A country of illegals, who follow not the rules!
Stand up and make a difference!

Beware of those playing loose with the truth!

Tzemin
Ition
Tsai

Dr. Tzemin Ition Tsai (蔡澤民博士) was born in Republic of China, in 1957. He holds a Ph.D. in Chemical Engineering and two Masters of Science in Applied Mathematics and Chemical Engineering. He is a professor at Asia University (Taiwan), editor of "Reading, Writing and Teaching" academic text. He also writes the long-term columns for Chinese Language Monthly in Taiwan.

He is a scholar with a wide range of expertise, while maintaining a common and positive interest in science, engineering and literature member.

He has won many national literary awards. His literary works have been anthologized and published in books, journals, and newspapers in more than 40 countries and have been translated into more than a dozen languages.

Before Sunset

Tomorrow has been waiting
Deeply extending to the Arabian Sea
That mountain edges are my supports and malicious
concealments too
I won't begin to surface my fatigue before now
More not allowed you to come
Although I am about to disappear
Black wilderness
Responding to The Land of Punt
Leave silently with the wind
The iridescent Clouds are still willing to act as my crown
Golden-winged grosbeaks vying for food on the branches

I will definitely come back
Like the Speke's gazelles at the foot of the mountain
The flower has begun to close
The clouds were no longer clearly defined
Under full will
Equidistant distance from the equator and the Tropic of
Cancer
Horn of Africa
My last light today
Will shoot to Kilmia
Cushitic, our words
Will continue to gallop in this Bilad al Barbar

Kiss

Beautiful body beside curly hair
Breast, The world is so sensitive
Induced love in the passion
Naked Mirage, under the pituitary gland
One by one
Look at the moving face with excitement
Keep up
A deeper temptation await
Completely surrender and unable to extricate themselves
Born too early so much
Mother-like supple
No intention to be your lover
Wait
Completely melted in the mouth, One day
Only when the infinite passion
Love is bleak, floating in the air
Before sealing
Sufficient
Has been living in the perceptual illusion

Those Barbarian Beauties

Brilliant Color clothing, RUBIK stealth in the group of
beauties
Rotation layers, aligned grids, leisurely dance
The small square, Miss POCKET
Twisting her waist, petite but indulge in emotions
The dance of the box,
always like to earn people's exclamations again and again

PROFESSOR's and V-FAMILY's sisters rush on like a
swarm of hornets
comes in a continuous stream, vie with others for glamor
Who should I lose my heart to?
In this festival, who is the Queen?
Mature charm, plump the body and prettily are all can't
keep anything to itself

Increased one more surface, PENTAGON
Magic belong to PYRAMIN
Sliding that snake-like skin, MASTERMORPHIX
Crossing the ridge, FISHER
All with obscure axioms waiting to be conquered

How wonderful my concubines
How beautiful these cubes are
Dance the breath of life in the spring
In that kneading, feeding that playfulness has to touchdown
Preoccupied In my Rubik's Cubes

Notes : *Rubik's Cubes, in my feelings, like the combination
of mathematics and magic, are an incredibly beautiful art,
long-term comfort my heart, when I need to calm down.
RUBIK, Miss POCKET, PROFESSOR, V-FAMILY,
PENTAGON, PYRAMIN , MASTERMORPHIX and
FISHER, as mentioned in this poems, all are the names of
each kinds of special shape of the Rubik's Cubes.*

Shareef
Abdur
Rasheed

Shareef Abdur Rasheed

Shareef Abdur-Rasheed, AKA Zakir Flo was born and raised in Brooklyn, New York. His education includes Brooklyn College, Suffolk County Community College and Makkah, Saudi Arabia. He is a Veteran of the Viet Nam era, where in 1969 he reverted to his now reverently embraced Islamic Faith. He is very active in the Islamic community and beyond with his teachings, activism and his humanity.

Shareef's spiritual expression comes through the persona of "Zakir Flo" . Zakir is Arabic for "To remind". Never silent, Shareef Abdur-Rasheed is always dropping science, love, consciousness and signs of the time in rhyme.

Shareef is the Patriarch of the Abdur-Rasheed Family with 9 Children (6 Sons and 3 Daughters) and 41 Grandchildren (24 Boys and 17 Girls).

For more information about Shareef, visit his personal FaceBook Page at :

https://www.facebook.com/shareef.abdurrasheed1
https://zakirflo.wordpress.com

Horn

----
of Africa
Ethiopia
Eritrea
Somalia
Djibouti
1,883,757 km
122,618,170
inhabitants
diverse
rich history
Ethiopia was
Habesha
Abyssinia
emperor Najasi
gave refuge to
Muslim's fleeing
tyranny in Hijaz
Arabia ruled by idol
worshipers
persecuted them
who worshiped only one
Allah(swt) 7th century
Haile Selassie emerged
victorious against invaders
from Italy 1941
addressed league of nations
became sensation 1935
Somalia standing strong
Mogadishu city of Islam
northeast Africa extends
hundreds of kilometers
into Arabian Sea

east-most projection of
African continent
Arabic, Somali, Tigrinya,
Afar, Wolaytta, English
Islam, Christianity, Judaism,
traditional
the horn is vast, array
of people's, cultures, tongues,
beliefs = horn of Africa

Metaphors

----

dance a creative expression
designed to capture
all that is love, beauty, life
but then comes dance troupe
from hell
bringing, ringing
Shaitan's bell
it summons, alerting
evil jinns to descend
wreaking havoc,
bringing mayhem,
death,
destruction,
love covered with
appears to be mud
is actually dung
beauty eradicated
ugly takes hold of souls
everything becomes
something bought, sold
quickly same ol $#!+ grows old
give me a metaphor for despair
but then again on second thought
don't want it,
don't need it anywhere near
to tear at
fabric of essence
that which illuminates bright
drives devil, jinns away in fright
to where dem dwell
awaiting inevitable hell
dem who thrive in darkness

metaphor for ignorance,
intolerance
enlightenment
much more relevant to life
enhance the chance to dance
in heaven

food4thought = education

all for 5 minutes . . . you 4real?
----
that's all this life got in it
but dem run a muck
like dem just don't give a
- - - -
but in all of 5 minutes
jigg is up
you done gave everything
for a 5 min. fling
lady 5 roasted you alive
cause you went for okay doke
believed the lie
you really think we're put here
indulge in waste, running to
catch mirages all day
that which is D.O.A.
dead on arrival
played your everlasting survival
so wipe that smile off your face
you who lived in haste
gave up honor for disgrace
you ain't gonna smile
when you lay in that grave awhile
and realize what wasn't with you
is your pile you hoarded up
now it's time to fess up
since you dissed the bless up
you went for the 5 min. thing
messed up
found out to late, nothing in it
as for forever in bliss
you thought you was to cleaver
for righteousness

ya'll about scratching the itch
for a 5 min. trip
now ain't that bout a bitch
sure wasn't worth giving up
eternal bliss
all for 5 minutes
you 4real?

food4thought = education

Kimberly Burnham

Kimberly Burnham

Find yourself in the pattern. As a 28-year-old photographer, Kimberly Burnham appreciated beauty. Then an ophthalmologist diagnosed her with a genetic eye condition saying, "Consider life, if you become blind." She discovered a healing path with insight, magnificence, and vision. Today, 33 years later, a poet and neurosciences expert with a PhD in Integrative Medicine, Kimberly's life mission is to change the global face of brain health. Using health coaching, Reiki, Matrix Energetics, craniosacral therapy, acupressure, and energy medicine, she supports people in their healing from brain, nervous system, and chronic pain issues. As managing editor of Inner Child Magazine, Kimberly's 2019 project is peace, language, and visionary poetry with her recently published book, *Awakenings: Peace Dictionary, Language and the Mind, a Daily Brain Health Program.*

http://www.NerveWhisperer.Solutions
https://www.linkedin.com/in/kimberlyburnham

No Boundaries of Otherness

The Guji people of the Horn of Africa
do not create boundaries of otherness
between themselves and non-humans
in day-to-day conversations

We give priority to "nagaya" peace in Afar
with livestock, children and our surroundings
all forms
living and non-living beings

We say "alaa manni nagayaa?"
an inquiry as to the peace and wellbeing
inside and outside
not of space but of relationship

"Mana" is the home
the inside
includes humans and livestock
with Ayyana spirits

The "alaa" or outside touches on
wild animals, forests and rivers
all living and nonliving things
with which the Guji connect

Abstractly inside is the invisible
the internal peace of the human mind
outside are visible creatures
we experience inner and outer equally important

Acceptance

Peace may start with "aqbal keen"
the acceptance of an idea in Somali

Peace "nabáda" may be set in motion by one
"arrin keen" one who initiates an idea

Tranquility may be launched with a call for peace
"baaqnabadeed"

Peace may begin with "booga dhayid"
healing the wounds and recovering

Calm may be made with words
"nabadeyn" peace making

Important Peace

In Harari spoken in Ethiopia
peace is said "sālam" and "amān"
"amān-be" means well or correctly
in peace and safety
a farewell greeting "amān-be"
literally an invocation to spend the night well
while repeating this word
"amān amān" means important
as if doubling down on peace is vital
for all of us to sleep well

Elizabeth E. Castillo

Elizabeth Esguerra Castillo

Elizabeth Esguerra Castillo is a multi-awarded and an Internationally-Published Contemporary Author/Poet and a Professional Writer / Creative Writer / Feature Writer / Journalist / Travel Writer from the Philippines. She has 2 published books, "Seasons of Emotions" (UK) and "Inner Reflections of the Muse", (USA). Elizabeth is also a co-author to more than 60 international anthologies in the USA, Canada, UK, Romania, India. She is a Contributing Editor of Inner Child Magazine, USA and an Advisory Board Member of Reflection Magazine, an international literary magazine. She is a member of the American Authors Association (AAA) and PEN International.

Web links:

Facebook Fan Page

https://free.facebook.com/ElizabethEsguerraCastillo

Google Plus

https://plus.google.com/u/0/+ElizabethCastillo

Amhara

Along the plains of Yemen
Their origins can be traced
Ancient Semitic people in Ethiopia,
Abyssinians, they are also called.

Said to be from the tribe of Shem,
Descendant of Yoktan
There are stories left untold
Depicting this eclectic people.

History tells Amhara people's roots
Mark to Menelik I, child of
The Immortal Lovers, Queen Sheba and King Solomon,
With their religion and tradition
Inherited from Axum.

Epitome of Real Beauty

one which was borne out of the world's madness
or a natural elegant beauty no need of sheer disguises?
a graceful lady in the throes of a newly found love,
blushing cheeks as sweet memories takes her to heights
    above.

one who never sulks out of life's biggest jokes at times
be there cloudy days today, she knows tomorrow would be
    sunshine
a lovely face to behold while you're having a ragged day,
a cheerful presence out of the blue she comes your way.

a sweet melody she often hums her way in a dreary room
gives you hope when everything else falters in a gloom
a faithful friend who accepts your flaws and loves you each
    day,
inner beauty that comes from within, won't easily fade
    away!

Oneness in the World

I am for unity and oneness in the world
I am against division all because of one's race, color, skin,
gender, nationality, and ideologies
In a world full of discrimination everywhere we lay our
eyes on,
Disparity among mankind is but an ugly depiction of a
changing world.

Despite one's color, one must be embraced and accepted
among a flock of different souls
You and I are brothers and sisters even if we are born in far
different continents
For we belong to one definite Oneness in the Universe,
You and I came from the same old origin of life.

Oneness in the world, will this just be merely a dream?
The choice is ours to take if we agree to respect and
embrace each other despite our many differences
Oneness in the world, will you be joining my advocacy of
promoting unity among nations?
Oneness in the world is what the world needs now, the
choice is ours somehow.

Joe
Paire

Joe Paire

Joseph L Paire' aka Joe DaVerbal Minddancer . . .
is a quiet man, born in a time where civil liberties
were a walk on thin ice. He's been a victim of his
own shyness often sidelined in his own quest for
love. He became the observer, charting life's path.
Taking note of the why, people do what they do. His
writings oft times strike a cord with the
dormant strings of the reader. His pen the rosined
bow drawn across the mind. He comes full-frontal
or in the subtlest way, always expressing in a way
that stimulate the senses.

www.facebook.com/joe.minddancer

Around The Horn

I bring Gold, Frankincense and Myrrh
Gift of the Magi with a hint of cinnamon
What place is this that borders water
Yet compassion dries out in the Red sea
Whom shall be King?

I bless the gatherers of natures gift
Can we just enjoy the fruits of this region
So many see them and seize them from free men
Please men a little sunset on the Jubba
Whom shall be King?

 I see a new form shaped like the mythical unicorn
A broken land mass formed to predict mans path
What path allows the time to savor such beauty?
Is it man's duty to rule the men who do vile things
Whom shall be King?

As The Sunsets

A day of praise and worship
Some of you rise without honoring yourselves

Time in glory or time in the limelight
History shows you get what you give
Existential dribble drooling over kibble

Some days you just have to meditate
Use what faith you have left in you
Never mind that never mind
Somethings asked are answered
Evening comes and you want to get away
Take a moment and sum up your day
Sunday evening are you grieving tomorrow
Are you leaving tomorrow
What's your reason for sorrow
Sunrise sunset and not a memory between them
I simply love just seeing them

Life In July

It's hard to frame a picture without a reference
How can one celebrate their deliverance
Freedom is a term from emotional phycology
I want to preform my apology
I'm sorry it's too hot for you
I'm sorry this month is not for you
Sparklers and red glare sulfur in the air
I can't breathe, I can't breathe
I can't stress enough the duress for a breath of fresh air

It's 5:00 am and it's my only chance to sit still
I match the stagnant air as shadows grow
No soul to share (is it hot enough for you)
maybe the rabbit in my yard can smell the coffee
The birds sure as heck express themselves quite loud
Humming birds feed in metallic green flashes
I'm starting to get an image now
Brain being canvas, vision being pen
I write July to end

hülya

n.

yılmaz

A retired Liberal Arts professor, hülya n. yılmaz [sic] is Co-Chair and Director of Editing Services at Inner Child Press International, and a literary translator. Her poetry has been published in an excess of sixty anthologies of global endeavors. Two of her poems are permanently installed in *TelePoem Booth*, a nation-wide public art exhibition in the U.S. She has shared her work in Kosovo, Canada, Jordan and Tunisia. hülya has been honored with a 2018 WIN Award of British Colombia, Canada. She is presently working on three poetry books and a short-story collection. hülya finds it vital for everyone to understand a deeper sense of self and writes creatively to attain a comprehensive awareness for and development of our humanity.

hülya n. yılmaz, Ph.D.

Writing Web Site
hulyanyilmaz.com

Editing Web Site
hulyasfreelancing.com

Incredible Richness

Ten different tongues – in Djibouti alone,
Fourteen in Eritrea, ninety in Ethiopia,
Yes, nine-ty – not a mere nine,
And fifteen in Somalia,
With most people in the Horn
Communicating within the language family
Of the Afroasiatic tongue, or better yet,
Utilizing its Cushitic or Semitic branches.
Sources declare: They all speak so fine
And maintain their level of enriched harmony.

Confusing?
Awe-inspiring?
Mind-boggling?

Three foreign tongues,
Or rather acquiring each
Took up my entire long-enough life.
Though that quest was not much of a strife,
There were challenges, mind you, on the side.
With whom to communicate through them
Was, in retrospect, the primary internal drive.
Not even nearly as many people on Earth
As the indigenous people of the Horn of Africa,
All of whom are evidenced to be in linguistic and ethnic
Sync. What a heart-soothing, hope-rising concept!
One is left to feel utterly inept . . .

I then wonder what their cultural richness is like . . .
It cannot be anything but utter delight.

We Owe Them . . .

Writing systems . . .
We take them for granted.
We sit down in front of a writing gadget,
And just write away. Write, write, write and write.
We tend not to pause to consider how is it, why is it
That we *can* write. Indigenous writing systems. The key!
We refuse the existence of an us-enabling script,
One that existed for at least 2000 years. The Ge'ez.
We do not even bother to look back to note the design
Of Osmanya, an alphabet of high phonetic sophistication,
One that had come to life in the mind
And through the capable hands of
Osman Yusuf Kenadid,
A Somali poet.

Writing
Poetry . . . ahhh!
The key to sanity within humanity!

In gratitude to Osman Yusuf Kenadid for his Ge'ez
And Nuruddin Farah – the celebrated writer of Somalia,
One with prestigious awards for his masterpieces of prose,
I humbly remain a lover of this burrowed ability
To write poetry, even if it is only
To maintain my own sanity
Within humanity!

Turkish Coffee Anyone?

Next time when I reach for my shiny Cezve and tiny Fincan
To indulge myself in the incomparable, mesmerizing
Aroma of Turkish Coffee and its enchanting taste,
I will bow down in honor of the land
That gave us those beans
To take my delight in:
Ethiopia.

Ethiopia: Your birthing of countless achievements
In countless fields of human advancement at large
Is not forgotten. Oh no!
Forgive my harmless addiction!
I know it can cause me some serious affliction,
But I just have to have my Turkish Coffee to sip,
For then, there is no need for another muddy dip . . .
If not every day, at least seven times a week.
Oh, I know! I do know that I am quite weak,
But, if prepared with TLC to make it gently right
And consumed with the required amount of might,
A smallest Fincan of Ethiopia-gifted Turkish Coffee
Will show off its meant-to-be position: Fully upright.

Teresa E. Gallion

Teresa E. Gallion

Teresa E. Gallion was born in Shreveport, Louisiana and moved to Illinois at the age of 15. She completed her undergraduate training at the University of Illinois Chicago and received her master's degree in Psychology from Bowling Green State University in Ohio. She retired from New Mexico state government in 2012.

She moved to New Mexico in 1987. While writing sporadically for many years, in 1998 she started reading her work in the local Albuquerque poetry community. She has been a featured reader at local coffee houses, bookstores, art galleries, museums, libraries, Outpost Performance Space, the Route 66 Festival in 2001 and the State of Oklahoma's Poetry Festival in Cheyenne, Oklahoma in 2004. She occasionally hosts an open mic.

Teresa's work is published in numerous Journals and anthologies. She has two CDs: *On the Wings of the Wind* and *Poems from Chasing Light*. She has published three books: *Walking Sacred Ground, Contemplation in the High Desert* and *Chasing Light*.

Chasing Light was a finalist in the 2013 New Mexico/Arizona Book Awards.

The surreal high desert landscape and her personal spiritual journey influence the writing of this Albuquerque poet. When she is not writing, she is committed to hiking the enchanted landscapes of New Mexico. You may preview her work at

http://bit.ly/1aIVPNq or *http://bit.ly/13IMLGh*

African Horn

The horn is a peninsula that kisses
the Arabian Sea in northeastern Africa.
The countries of the Horn of Africa
are culturally diverse in achievements
in agriculture, architecture, art, cuisine,
education, literature and music.

Ethiopia claims the earliest known use
of seed grass, first to use coffee
and known for its unique music.
Somalia is known for literature through
significant writers in the modern era.

The diverse and talented people of the Horn
impacted by mellineums of outside intrusion
find themselves living in poverty and chaos
blended with violence in today's social scheme.

Catch and Release

Her soul waits with patience.
Watches her shatter mirrors
overtime, hide behind curtains,
hands bleeding.

One day the pain forces her
to look around the curtain.
An eagle captures fear
and takes it away.

She feels a burst of freedom,
runs beyond the curtain,
sees the birds for the first time
sailing on the breeze.

Gold Belt

Pain, scars, sagging body,
wrinkle waves are living marks,
Notches on the golden belt
you wear today.

Wear your belt with gratitude.
Let your smile expand its glow.
Spray kindness into the universe.
Watch love blossoms land
on heads of the needy.

You know you arrived
in the present moment when
your smile touches the heart
of another and they smile
without knowing why.

Ashok K. Bhargava

Ashok K. Bhargava

Ashok Bhargava is a poet, writer, community activist, public speaker, management consultant and a keen photographer. Based in Vancouver, he has published several collections of his poems: Riding the Tide, Mirror of Dreams, A Kernel of Truth, Skipping Stones, Half Open Door and Lost in the Morning Calm. His poetry has been published in various literary magazines and anthologies.

Ashok is a Poet Laureate and poet ambassador to Japan, Korea and India. He is founder of WIN: Writers International Network Canada. Its main objective is to inspire, encourage, promote and recognize writers of diverse genres, artists and community leaders. He has received many accolades including Nehru Humanitarian Award for his leadership of Writers International Network Canada, Poets without Borders Peace Award for his journeys across the globe to celebrate peace and to create alliances with poets, and Kalidasa Award for creative writings.

Horn of Africa

An ancient land of thirsty
soil and luscious souls,
baked in bright sunrays.

Life begins, life ends,
life gives into life here,
flowing, as on wings

giving
and receiving
in a continuous motion.

You rise to
the spirit of drums,
the melody of resurgence,

a bold survivor,
there are no words
to praise your resilience.

Eritrea

A sudden newness
dawns on me.

I notice
I have become a bird.

My body is lighter now
and my bones hollow.

I can fly
defy gravity.

My age is only a number and
I love my new incarnation.

It would've driven me insane
a few years ago.

Now I appreciate it
and love my lover moon.

Ashok K. Bhargava

Waiting

I have many
ups and downs
many lovers and admirers
since you abandoned me.

Someday, if you come back
you will find me
still the way you
left me, waiting.

May be you will find
few wrinkles on my face
few white Hair, other than you
I'm too tired to think...

Caroline
'Ceri Naz'
Nazareno

Carolin 'Ceri' Nazareno

Caroline Nazareno-Gabis a.k.a. Ceri Naz, born in Anda, Pangasinan known as a 'poet of peace and friendship', is a multi-awarded poet, journalist, editor, publicist, linguist, educator, and women's advocate.

Graduated cum laude with the degree of Bachelor of Elementary Education, specialized in General Science at Pangasinan State University. Ceri have been a voracious researcher in various arts, science and literature. She volunteered in Richmond Multicultural Concerns Society, TELUS World Science, Vancouver Art Gallery, and Vancouver Aquarium.

She was privileged to be chosen as one of the Directors of Writers Capital International Foundation (WCIF), Member of the Poetry Posse, one of the Board of Directors of Galaktika ATUNIS Magazine based in Albania; the World Poetry Canada and International Director to Philippines; Global Citizen's Initiatives Member, Association for Women's rights in Development (AWID) and Anacbanua. She has been a 4th Placer in World Union of Poets Poetry Prize 2016, Writers International Network-Canada ''Amazing Poet 2015'', The Frang Bardhi Literary Prize 2014 (Albania), the sair-gazeteci or Poet-Journalist Award 2014 (Tuzla, Istanbul, Turkey) and World Poetry Empowered Poet 2013 (Vancouver, Canada).

HOA's Wind of Hope

Djibouti,
Salt of the eastern coast,
Life-blood of the insurgents,
Etched historical links to Issas and Afars ,
Amidst the cold revolts and war,
Djibouti's beauty remained, it was never thawed.

Eritrea,
Its name is deeper as the Red Sea,
Urheimat, the original homeland
Of kingdoms and empires,
The mosques offered flowers,
Blossomed exposé and freedom.

Ethiopia,
Landlocked dynasty of Queen of Sheba,
Its highlands and mountain ranges,
Are the embodiment of Abyssinia's dream,
 Elevation of full sovereignty,
The new flower's dance.

Somalia,
The Land of Punt,
Keepers of Myyrh and frankincense,
Flanked of cinnamon and spices,
Just like its influence
To the people,
The home of peacemakers.

a walk of purpose

raising the flag
red, blue, white and yellow
red for courage, not bloody revolts
blue for peace, not wars and bombings,
white for purity of heart, not messy evildoings,
yellow for enlightenment, not blackout of freedom,
freedom of expression,
freedom of the people and for the people,
raise the flag,
a walk of respect,
woven for a territory,
sovereignty,
and identity.

quatriemme

crystal clear that was
while bathing on the
sunset's kisses
where ponds, rivers
and lakes of love
took away the flaws,
your heart's sunshine
to eternity's quest;
that single day
was a world
of ours, my love, forever.

Swapna
Behera

Swapna Behera is a bilingual contemporary poet, author, translator and editor from Odisha, India .She was a teacher from 1984 to 2015 . Her stories, poems and articles are widely published in National and International journals, and ezines, and are translated into different national and International languages. She has penned four books. She was conferred upon the Prestigious International Poesis Award of Honor at the 2nd Bharat Award for Literature as Jury in 2015, The Enchanting Muse Award in India World Poetree Festival 2017, World Icon of Peace Award in 2017, and the Pentasi B World Fellow Poet in 2017.. She is the recipient of Gold Cross Of Wisdom Award ,the medal for The Best Teachers of the World from World Union of Poets in 2018, and The LIfe time Achievement Award ,The Best Planner Award, The Sahitya Shiromani Award, ATAL BiHARI BAJPAYEE AWARD 2018, Ambassador De Literature Award 2018 .She is the Ambassador of Humanity by Hafrikan Prince Art World Africa 2018 and an official member of World Nation's Writers Union ,Kazakhstan2018. At present she is the manager at Large, Planner and Columnist of The Literati, the administrator of several poetic groups ,the member of the Special Council of Five of World Union of Poets and the Cultural Ambassador of Inner Child Press U.S.

Swapna Behera

<u>3 poems for July</u>

I pray for the magic moment

I pray
for the magic moment, mama
a moment
when I can have
cassava porridge on my plate
we can eat together
under the sky
to celebrate moonlit
I will play nasaro of grand father

We shall have toilets and water
You need not have to run
miles to get water everyday
We shall have our own mundals
I wish to pay football, mama
I am your lovely daughter

I don't need star
or gold coin on my palm
just a blanket as I shiver in cold nights
I need sanitary napkins, mama

we will not speak habaar
and last but not the least
please don't sell me
to the tall man of that village
I don't want to be his wife,
I am only twelve, mama
I don't want to massage his three wives
and cook for the family of twelve

I want to play pebbles ...
I love my soil, my own Somalia
here forests are green
I wish to smile still greener ......
give me my smile .... I pray mama..........

Mundals are permanent structures houses made of mud and
dung mixture
Nasaro is the high ritual drum
We will not speak habaar
Habaars are ill wish

The Adolescent Fossil

The adolescent fossil screams

obstinate arguments in the ether

don't ever discard a calendar

the somersault

to rupture and bloom

spread the periphery

rather

write the post script

of a sapling

Guarantee of a script

who can guarantee a script?
a script is always volatile
takes momentum
when you wish to be silent
a music in a flute
that blows seas infinity ....

does it ever dissolve the shadows?
guarantee of a script is
refined bark of every tree
a command of alphabets
that bends as the spine of a farmer
who grows corn in a desert?

invisible scripts are golden kites
meditation and monologues
approaching dawn
a hyphen between life and death

dusks are visible as
darkness is also
a celebration to introspect
than glittering lights
you struggle, suffocate
swim, sail and finally dance
to feel light
a script is guaranteed
becomes a language
a value, a bliss
when lips and hearts mingle
to weave a new sky

Swapna Behera

Albert 'Infinite' Carrasco

I'm a project life philanthropist, I speak about the non ethical treatment of poor ghetto people. Why? My family was their equal, my great grandmother and great grandfather was poor, my grandmother and grandfather, my mother and father, poverty to my family was a sequel, a traditional Inheritance of the subliminal. I paid attention to the decades of regression, i tried to make change, but when I came to the fork in the road and looked at the signs that read wrong < > right, I chose the left, the wrong direction, because of street life interactions a lot around me met death or incarceration. I failed myself and others. I regret my decisions, I can't reincarnate dead men, but I can give written visions in laymens. I'm back at that fork in the road, instead of it saying wrong or right, I changed it, now it says dead men < > life.

Infinite poetry @lulu.com

Alcarrasco2 on YouTube

Infinite the poet on reverbnation

Infinite Poetry

http://www.lulu.com/us/en/shop/al-infinite-carrasco/infinite-poetry/paperback/product-21040240.html

Horn of Africa

Welcome to the land of Barbara and Habesha.
Djibouti, Eritrea, Ethiopia and Somalia,
The easternmost projection of Africa.
The people converse in mainly in Amharic, Oromo and
Somali,
Other languages spoken are English, Arabic, French and
Italian.
Islam, Christianity and Judaism are the most common
religions.
Architectural wonders include Monolithic Obelisks like
King Ezana's Stela
The Citadel,
The Sultanate of Adal in Zeila
along with Fasilides castle in Gondar.
You'll be awe looking in the capital of Ethiopia, Addis
Ababa,
Just as you will witnessing the UNESCO world heritage
site at Lalibela.

Urban poetry

People that haven't seen or heard from in a long time bug when they hear that I'm a poet with urban bars, they're used to me stretch'n when I'm chef'n and bust'n when cats start front'n, They didn't know I could scratch off scabs and instantly bleed scars. Coagulation narrations. Every time I grab a pen I relive the past, Poor days, rich times and flatlines from bloodbaths. Being able to story tell is a gift gained from living in hell amongst mixn, cuttn, cheffn, bustn semis without leaving shells and how not to get caught makn directs or observation sales. I'm just being honest, inf will always be one of the hardest regardless to the fact I no longer see the blacksmiths and re-up on what guerrillas harvest. I go back to the times of holes in walls, stamp and cap color wars, trapped up grocery stores, counting stacks of money from waistlines to the floor and all the way up to now where I hardly see a familiar face anymore. The in betweens are tragic... addictions, football number bids and caskets. My past of drugs, guns and murder became my written and spoke'n genre. All the time spent in the trenches with my A alike brothers made me a seasoned vet, professional mourner and author. Shedding light on darkness is my aim, because young playas hear all the pros and none of the cons of the game.

Inner voices

When I was angry I trained myself to stay home, I knew the first dude that got out of line will get lined up by blue or chrome. Had anger issues because of living in poverty, living with a slug in me and because the root of all evil took a lot of my people and I can't shake the look of their wives and mothers crying, blowing snot in tissue, looking at reality and wishing it wasn't true. I kept pushn for those that was still here while mourning those around me in the shape of air. I had to deal with good and bad voices when I was tight. Inf walk away... Bellaco show em the light. Inf ya got a lot to lose... bellaco wet shit up, show em how you move. I had to let time pass in meditation so I don't make bad decisions due to emotion by listening to the "bad" conversation. I'm a survivor of a kill or be killed era, had to be ready whenever and wherever, it didn't matter the caliber, it was all about who's aim was better, it's a cold cold world, I just adjusted with the weather, that's why when there's any kind of drama temptation immediately tries to take over. Bellaco it's water...

.

Eliza Segiet

Eliza Segioet

After earning a Master's Degree in Philosophy at the Jagiellonian University in Krakaw, Poland, Eliza Segiet proceeded with her post-graduate studies in the fields of Cultural Knowledge, Penal Revenue and Economic Criminal Law, Arts and Literature and Film and Television Production in the Polish city, Lodz.

With specific regard to her creative writings, the author describes herself as being torn in her passion for engaging in two literary genres: Poetry and Drama. A similar dichotomy from within is reflected on Segiet's own words about her true nature: She likes to look at the clouds, but she keeps both of her feet set firmly on the ground.

The author describes her worldview as being in harmony with that of Arthur Schopenhauer: "Ordinary people merely think how they shall 'spend' their time; a man of talent tries to 'use' it".

Eliza Segiet

Mother Nature
translated from Polish by Artur Komoter

Where
the salty lakes
hide their springs,
where
the earth
shows its life
– enchanted we congeal.
The magic of colors is happening.

Dallol fascinates,
the Afars see it every day.

The hopes do not languish
that one day,
not yet stripped of beauty,
the terrestrial extraterrestrial patch
of the world
will delight not only the natives
but those who will visit this place
and not leave behind
civilizational monuments
of their own stupidity.

Everyday
translated from Polish by Artur Komoter

When
you leave everyday life far behind,
so you can wait out the bad times here,
comes alive in you
the memory:
of the cloudy sky
and beautiful moments of forgetfulness.

Although memories and plans
cross with each other –
you know
that nothing will be like
it was yesterday.

Always repeat:
it was good that I was here.

Tomorrow, it may surprise you.

This Moment
translated from Polish by Artur Komoter

Ready for happiness,

we greedily go towards it.

And when it opens like a

dawn-awakened nenuphar,

it is not because

it will always be so,

but in order to enjoy

this moment.

William S. Peters Sr.

Bill's writing career spans a period of over 50 years. Being first Published in 1972, Bill has since went on to Author in excess of 40 additional Volumes of Poetry, Short Stories, etc., expressing his thoughts on matters of the Heart, Spirit, Consciousness and Humanity. His primary focus is that of Love, Peace and Understanding!

Bill says . . .

I have always likened Life to that of a Garden. So, for me, Life is simply about the Seeds we Sow and Nourish. All things we "Think and Do", will "Be" Cause and eventually manifest itself to being an "Effect" within our own personal "Existences" and "Experiences" . . . whether it be Fruit, Flowers, Weeds or Barren Landscapes! Bill highly regards the Fruits of his Labor and wishes that everyone would thus go on to plant "Lovely" Seeds on "Good Ground" in their own Gardens of Life!

to connect with Bill, he is all things Inner Child

www.iaminnerchild.com

Personal Web Site

www.iamjustbill.com

Let loose my horn

They grabbed her by the Horn
And proceeded to wrestle her
To the ground . . .
Yes, she shall rise again
And re-announce her prominence
As the flagship
Of creation

Her bowels are rich
With minerals, gold and culture
Still yet to be
Fully reconnoitered,
Negotiated,
Or exploited

Come back and take me
She bellows
Into the peninsula
Of life,
Come back
And see what riches
We have for you

Open thine eye . . .
Open thy heart . . .
And thy soul shall live . . . forever

Explore our mountains
Walk our valleys
Roll in our plains
And drink of our waters
While our Sun kisses you

Gently upon the lips
Of your dreams
Of civility

I beseech you O Seeker,
Come,
And I too shall kiss you with tenderness
Upon your weary brow
And we can resurrect ourselves
As one

Let loose my horn

The Game of Thrones

Dear Friends from the 'Quiet World'
Who speak not up
Of the wrong . . .
There will come a time
When 'Time' comes for you
And I am sure then
You will change your 'Silent Song'

You sit idly and comfortably by
Ignoring with ease the parade
As humanity moves forth
In celebrance
Towards perdition
As you play your games . . .
Charades

Oh, yes my friend
You too will not escape
Should the burning house come tumbling down . . .
But don't you worry nor fret my friend
We will let you keep your shine-less crown

So be content, for in the mean time
And embrace your 'Not Me' stance
When the music of truth begins to play
For the final time
You too are invited
To the dance

The fools have ruled the castle
Perhaps a bit too long my friend
Their dastardly deeds done in shadows
But when the light of truth comes to stay
They all shall meet their end

And should you wish to hold on
You can join them too
Cloaked in your indifference and ignorance
Given to you by the elitist few

The tail CAN NOT wag the dog
In spite of what you believe,
For we the people,
The bottom dwellers of your
Now failing world
Have conceived
And shall achieve
A new way,
A new thought,
A new humanity
That shall exemplify a love
For all . . . even you
In our new
Game of thrones

Absolute

Infusion
Illusion
Delusion
Conclusion

What Is God ?
Have You Seen Him Lately ?
Have you spoken with Him today ?

Absolute Belief
Offers absolute Relief
Absolutely

The miracles you seek
are yours to command
learn to demand
of your self
to open and receive
the fruits of what you believe
for you are free to conceive
incieve
achieve
that of your Heart's Desires
but you must tend the fire
and make sure it does not go out
when faced with your doubt
or the bouts
with the world of things

shed the tears
let go the fears
for they are of the World

for the world is built not
upon a rock
nor is it eternal
it is but
Infusion
Illusion
Delusion
Conclusion

which shall pass
as it always has
Absolutely

this brings forth the contusions
of our Souls
and the lesions
upon our hearts
that no longer feel
what it knows to be real

Absolute

William S. Peters, Sr.

July
2019

Featured Poets

~ * ~

Saadeddin Shahin

Alok Kumar Ray

Fahredin Shehu

Andy Scott

i FLY

because I Can

...said the Dreamer to the world.

Saadeddin Shahin

Saadeddin Shahin is a Jordanian poet, novelist, essayist and children literature writer.

He was born in Beit Jala, Palestine, on May 7, 1950. He started his career as a teacher, then a principal. He also served as a chief of social and psychological services, and a manager of students' affairs. Additionally, he founded an educational organization in Jordan of which he is currently the director. Shahin is a board member and vice president of Jordanian Writers Association (JWA). He is a member of Arab Writers Union, and Asian and African Writers' Union, He served as chief editor of *Awraq* Journal for several terms. In 1990 he founded the Ajneha (Wings) Band for Heritage and Culture.

He has published nine books of poetry, including *An Oasis Of Hope* (1993), *In The Notebook of The Dream* (1997), *The Heights Of Shadow* (1997), *I See What Yamama Saw* (2009), *Alone Save For The Shirt Of Songs* (2015), and *Innocent Bleeding*(2018). He has also published a novel entitled *Death Does Not Always Come* (2002).

Saadeddin Shahin

Details...

Translated from Arabic by : Dr. Sahar Khalil

Details of this bitter Absence dissolved me
Since I promised to slaughter the lambs which got fat
As seasons yet depart my realm ..
My ever lasting wonder
For what may hide in the Earth's fur
After wild winter's ploughs, of awaiting worries

Like a spilling dream came I
From a flower in withering sphere
And on the touch of fingers
I became a fossil in the heart ..
But sea did not cherish this Shine

Thus, cloned he waves after waves,
To through us in deep of the seas

Neither the Shark sharps his teeth
To behold our Beauty at the last Wedding ..
And swallow the Sacrifice Spittle
As folks feed their Joys, once to the huge ocean
And once to the deep of deeps

Nor the Whale opens a gate
For us to get rest, while its hollow carry us on
Towards a land, of arbours with season's grapes
Over whom we cross, wounded and hurt
So she grants our bodies to the dust ..

Like clouds, picked I came
When seasons ceased to exist

To reach out the point of all seas, who kidnapped my lust
All at once ..

And here I reach the rescue years
On the cairn of our dreams
Like some dervish and believers I prayed
That no other choice I had

It was my dissolve's details that I reached
And still, I didn't improvise my songs
Which stormed me much as I register them on the hymn of
the hearts of the poor

Outside the door stands a crew of hungry people
And behind the windows is the semen of our Dominants
They have their share, We must obey

Forced by heredity to have my blood
Chronic in my blood

I tamed my hand through the fingers
To slightly rub the match
And feel pity for it from the burn

Who can, then, light the tar in the sea gloominess?
So can the boats without me pass ..

Just as we, Lamps get bribed as well
Oils of food,
 tar,
and stoves
And so awake beacons from the lamp's dormancy

Like the sleep, are bribed with their dreams,
 longer they stay
But longer they lost

Saadeddin Shahin

Fond of women's neigh I am
Who made of their trills,
A map for Joy

Once, in the wedding of virgins
Another, when they seek to ride the Reversion
To the saddle of Death
When crowned with Martyrdom and promotion

Impressed by the wind
Who might whisper the Silence of the seas
To award the waves a song among the emptiness

Shut is the way to release
Merely belongs to release !

Now digital is this World
So dig in the heap of wind, and fetch my digit
Out from your archives
Thou who are deeply busy investigate !

Now, through this frothing Ether
Between my ink and my Molar

My digit is not hard in your possession
My voice now is only my whisper !

And here I swear in my Name
And in the Remedy's in the churches
And in our impregnable Verses and in my sacred Jerusalem
That uttered now
Is my own voice, my own sensation

It's all mine now
Do not overstrain with investigation

However, after every Elapse
I will declare that what you hear is only nonsense !

And that what lies in my mouth is a sting
As a pursued man in the territory of "Abs" *

---

* "Abs" was one of the most famous Arabic tribes with strong fighters in the past history.

Like an ancient door

Translated from Arabic by : Dr. Sahar Khalil

Like an ancient door
They step all mornings on my threshold
Then I listen
To the last passengers

Whenever a knocker stroke my wood
My ribs protest
Against me to the passengers

When few of them passed me, said to me;-
Sandalwood is mine
And that I am root natured
Others said:- waterwheels
On such this strider rounds

It is the Extreme
And embezzled crossing is now easy through ....
Before, all those who passed my threshold were
Bending if they wished to pass across

My woodworm gnawed me
I never believed but her
When she said:
You, door ....
You are nothing but a crossing terminal
But I have no sin except of
That I the door's wood rot

You door ! you can
Only still be an ancient door
a way
for the incomings to seek shield in your shadow
when they step the steps

when they pass their hands on the door over
what the good formers have left
and flow over into the under wing of the graves

out of you door, come out all brides at wedding
at you begins the line up
at the king's doors
starts the weak people bend

I never believed but her
And she goes on snorting me
And there she widely opens
Abyss in the wall leading to my attic
In the last passage

Little Bird.. sing
Translate from Arabic by : D . Sahar Khaleel

wrote this by the inspiration of a little bird on the riverbank
of Jordan's river by the baptism,
Drop by my grave ..
And mention do not wave
Infatuated he was, with poplar trees, by the fence of his
village ..

Carrying in his hands a little bird's repast
Who was gasping to cross the fence ..

Wind was hodgepodge of things ..
Most of glass ...

Feather of wings over wings..
Migrates to lands he just left

And draws among the pine trees
A melody song symbolize the lover's kiss

Thousand doors shut the wind
And .. Broke the bar!

fetch the nest when you return for its tune
And warble enough soon
To make every body hear
And between your hands every fain bends
And capricious wakes up

Oh little bird, warble as much as you can
So the nest on your lips will still be shown
Wherever folded you the ways of disperse

Alok Kumar Ray

Bio: Dr. Ray teaches political science to both undergraduate and postgraduate students. He is a bi-lingual poet and writes both in Odia and English. Many poems written by him have been published in a number of national and international journals, anthologies, tabloids and newsletters. He regularly contributes poems to a number of online poetry groups of repute. He resides at the district headquarters of Jagatsinghpur in the state of Odisha, India.

illusion

not a day dreamer i am
not a person who indulges in sarcasms
still then in wee hours of a fine morning
before birds could start chirping
dews could dazzle grasping golden morning sun
a surreal dream me before i could wake up
a nymph was dancing in the air
her flowerly vessel navigating the blue sky
velvety ambience engulfing the whole
fragrance of flowers mesmerizing the meadow
spinning she like a whirlwind
i was engrossed in deep ecstatic view
her alluring but crooked look, luscious lips
entangled me like the ring of satrun
her song was sweety, intoxicating
suddenly found i morning sun painted the sky in yellowish
    hue
went away she from my thought purview
sweat rolled on my forehead signaling fright
i discovered me in a meadow where the zyphr was leisurely
    blowing
so soothing the vicinity, i was surprised
suddenly i woke up drenched with anxiety
i found me in a bed ravaged by
rotten thought, very unrealistic

i am walking away

i walking away for greener pasture
i am walking away with painful gesture
i am walking away to rebuild my stature
some men are like straight line
they don't intersect but shine
i belong to this genre very fine

no place is there for compromise in my dictionary
its better to leave than to live sans essential glossary
i don't think life can be plagued by occasional treachery
i will revert back chasing cacophonous humdrum
i will set new goals amidst enchanting spectrum
treat this my dear as my last ultimatum

i have the required tenacity to embrace stride
your rancorous rues i will submerge being tide
life is a huge canvas to bring laurel if one deserts pride

imagination, take me there where i have never been

i am longing to live life of the countryside, unmindful of
    any rule of loss or gain to abide
want to play from morning to night, no restriction that may
    cause fright
with friends i will compete to catch butterflies, to get relief
    from defeat i will rely on cries
swim and sink in the nearby river, till parents browbeat to
    block my entry to home for ever
spend the whole night with friends sans parent's approval,
    in the morning come back home and face trial
ride up to top of the tree to pluck berry, falling down
    unluckily and bear minor injury
skip school and go the nearby fair, return in the evening
    and get thrashing by dad seems unfair
tear papers from notebooks to make paper boats very fancy,
    get ultimatum from teachers for delinquency
imagination, take me there where i have never been, being
    a city child which i have never seen

Fahredin Shehu

Fahredin Shehu is a writer, a critic, Independent Scientific Researcher in the fields of World Spiritual Heritage and Sacral Esthetics and a certified expert in Adult learning on the platforms of Capacity Building, Training, Coaching, Mentoring and Facilitating. A member of the European Academy of Poets and the Poetry Center at Roehampton University in London, Shehu is Director and Organizer of the Kosova International Poetry Festival.

Born in 1972 in Rahovec – South-East of Kosova, Shehu graduated from Prishtina University with a degree in Oriental Studies. Passionate about Calligraphy, he actively works on discovering new mediums and techniques for this specific form of plastic art.

Three Fives by Nine

5.

1. You said: "Be!" and it became six times
2. the repetition of foreign genetic code.
3. The red dice I throw in the Sea of Galilee.
4. I saw senile while drinking the last absolute of life.
5. Nard, Amber, Jasmine, Cedre, Horse skin.
6. I also made an elixir of aromas- to wait
7. thus that multiple wing light
8. to transport me to the below Arctic
9. and from there to the tears that I alone must smell

5.

1. We tried to get drunk by dews and by drunkenness
2. our wine turned blood, until we got sick and
3. searching for the diluted ecstasy. We remained intoxicated
4. as those in love in the eyes of whom is visible only
5. the star distance, while cheeks are wet by tears and turn
6. to nacre. Here we are oh you Giants of Soul,
7. the God's servants. Not like us, not like anyone else, but like you. The white
8. light while it enfolds you, while it covers
9. your rainbow color luminosity.

5.

1. I saw them crying and crying I felt
2. in suspicion shall I preserve this
3. stream of love for all
4. worlds in order to keep the freshness like
5. dew drops when they moisten a bending
6. grass-leaves. Doves observing and
7. butterflies with fluttering wings only
8. temporarily showing their beauty so to
9. leave their vestige like poets leaves their verses.

Andrew 'Andy' Scott

Andrew 'Andy' Scott

Andrew Scott is a native of Fredericton, NB. During his time as an active poet, Andrew Scott has taken the time to speak in front of a classrooms, judge poetry competitions as well as be published worldwide in such publications as The Art of Being Human, Battered Shadows and The Broken Ones. His books, ***Snake With A Flower, The Phoenix Has Risen, The Path, The Storm Is Coming*** and ***Through My Eyes*** are available now. ***Searching*** is his fifth poetry collection.

To contact Andrew, email …***andrewscott.scott@gmail.com***

http://twitter.com/JustMaritimeBoy

http://andrewmscott.com

http://www.facebook.com/andymscott

http://www.facebook.com/JustaMaritimeBoy

Paradise Gone

Rosie looks from a cracked sidewalk
that is covered in fresh soot
from the fresh, burned out home
that was once Rosie's.
Not even the wooden frame is left.
All taken by the hunger of a fire.
Flames that feasted,
leaving Rosie to stare, confused
at what to do with her dream, paradise gone.

Old Ned walks down the smoldering road
that is covered in the burnt remains
of the businesses that are no longer
in the once postcard town.
Now full of the colour of black and ash,
lined with shells of cars and trucks
that are now burned to a skeleton
of the once picturesque paradise, now gone.

Defeated firefighters laying motionless
in a make shift camp in a nearby town.
Thoughts of what they could not save.
The flames won the battle
against all they had.
The winds pushed the destruction
to a place where they had to surrender.
A retreat, leaving possessions and people behind.
Finding those that could not be saved.
Tears did not exhaust the flames
that continue to dance in their numb minds
for the rest of their and everyone's lives.
The paradise is gone.

Shaking In A Hole

Little Jane covers herself in a trusty blanket,
shielding herself from the sunlight
and the unpredictability of the outside world.

The worries about how others will see her.
Thoughts of how her clothes look.
Are the hair and make-up just right?
People are harsh within their eyes.

Little Jane worries about the front lawn
and how walker-bys see the flowers.
Poor husband has to weed each weekend
to get her to stop fretting about perfection.

An everyday job at the bakery
is the only time Jane goes out
even then the internal fight
to walk through those doors.

The days outside are too much,
inside is so much better
so no one can judge her
as Little Jane stares, shaking in her hole.

The Mutant

The explosion just happened.
I did not even feel anything
until I woke up four days later,
laying in a hospital bed.

The nurses and doctors tried to explain
as they dressed and undressed bandages
on my hot face as to why I was there.

The steam from a pressured pipe
burned the face and neck
after bursting while I was
being our home's plumber.
This is what I was told.
I remember nothing of that day.

The healing took months
with the skin graphs
to cover the burned portions
or what could be covered.

My face has the scars.
Red, blistered scars with lines.
I will never be able to hide them.
Not from the people that stare
when I am seen without a hat and hoodie
that is constantly hiding the evidence.

My workplace gave me a walled office
so others would not stop looking and talking
or so no one would see customers flinching.

My house has gotten quieter
as my partner left months
after I walked back through the door.
Affection was hard for her to give.
The sadness in her face said everything.
Do not blame her for getting affection elsewhere.

I sit in the dark a lot now
most of the time hoodie still on.
It is a habit now.
Hiding this mutant from even myself.

Remembering

our fallen soldiers of verse

Janet Perkins Caldwell
February 14, 1959 ~ September 20, 2016

Alan W. Jankowski
16 March 1961 ~ 10 March 2017

Coming
April 2020

The
World Healing, World Peace
International Poetry Symposium
Stay Tuned

for more information

intouch@innerchildpress.com

'building bridges of cultural understanding'
www.innerchildpress.com

144

Inner Child Press
News

Poetry Posse Members

We are so excited to share and announce a few of the current books, as well as the new and upcoming books of some of our Poetry Posse authors.

On the following pages we present to you ...

Jackie Davis Allen

Gail Weston Shazor

hülya n. yılmaz

Nizar Sartawi

Faleeha Hassan

Fahredin Shehu

Caroline 'Ceri' Nazareno

Eliza Segiet

William S. Peters, Sr.

Now Available at
www.innerchildpress.com

No Illusions

Through the Looking Glass

Jackie Davis Allen

Now Available at

www.innerchildpress.com

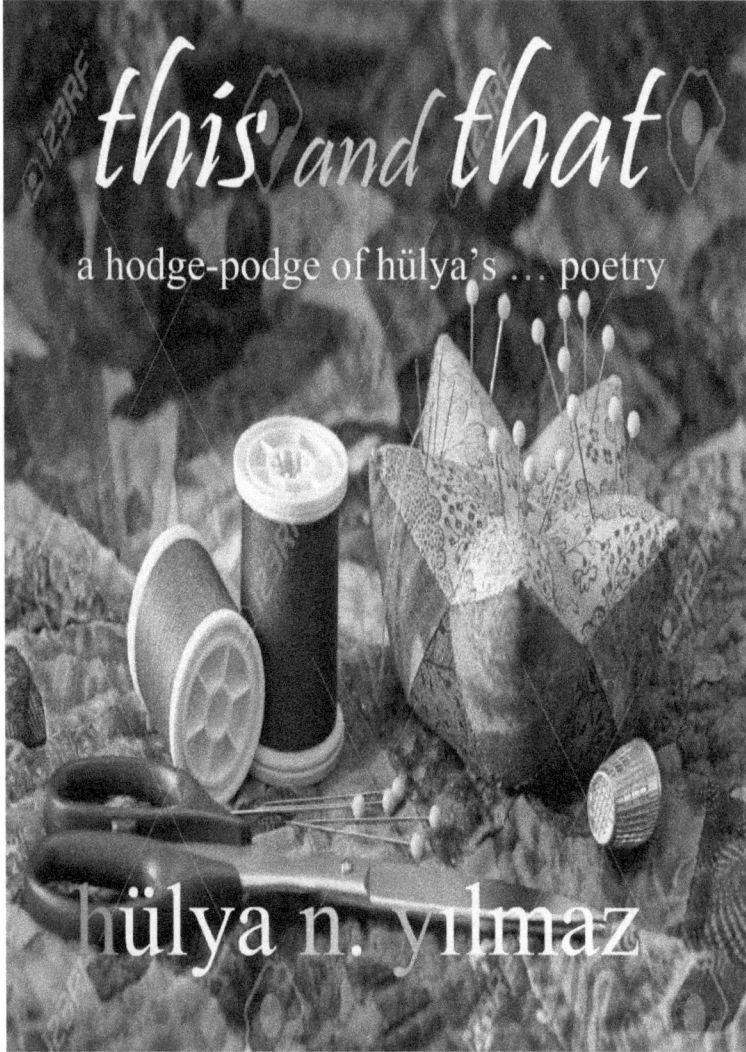

this and that

a hodge-podge of hülya's ... poetry

hülya n. yılmaz

Now Available at

www.innerchildpress.com

mommy i hear those whispers . . . again

WilliAM s. PeTers, sR.

Inner Child Press News

Now Available at
www.innerchildpress.com

HERENOW

FAHREDIN SHEHU

Now Available at
www.innerchildpress.com

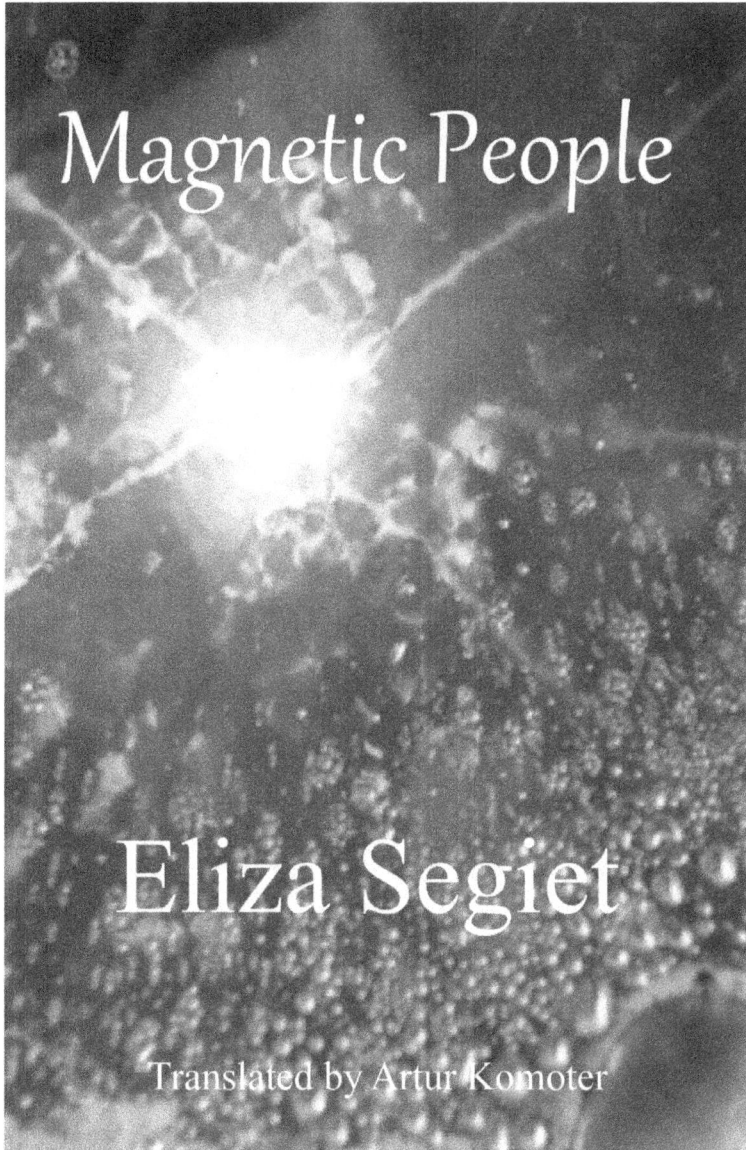

Magnetic People

Eliza Segiet

Translated by Artur Komoter

Now Available at
www.innerchildpress.com

Now Available at
www.innerchildpress.com

Lies
My
Grandfathers
Told
Me

Gail Weston Shazor

Now Available at
www.innerchildpress.com

Aflame

Memoirs in Verse

hülya n. yılmaz

Now Available at
www.innerchildpress.com

My Shadow

Nizar Sartawi

Now Available at
www.innerchildpress.com

Now Available at
www.innerchildpress.com

Breakfast

for

Butterflies

Faleeha Hassan

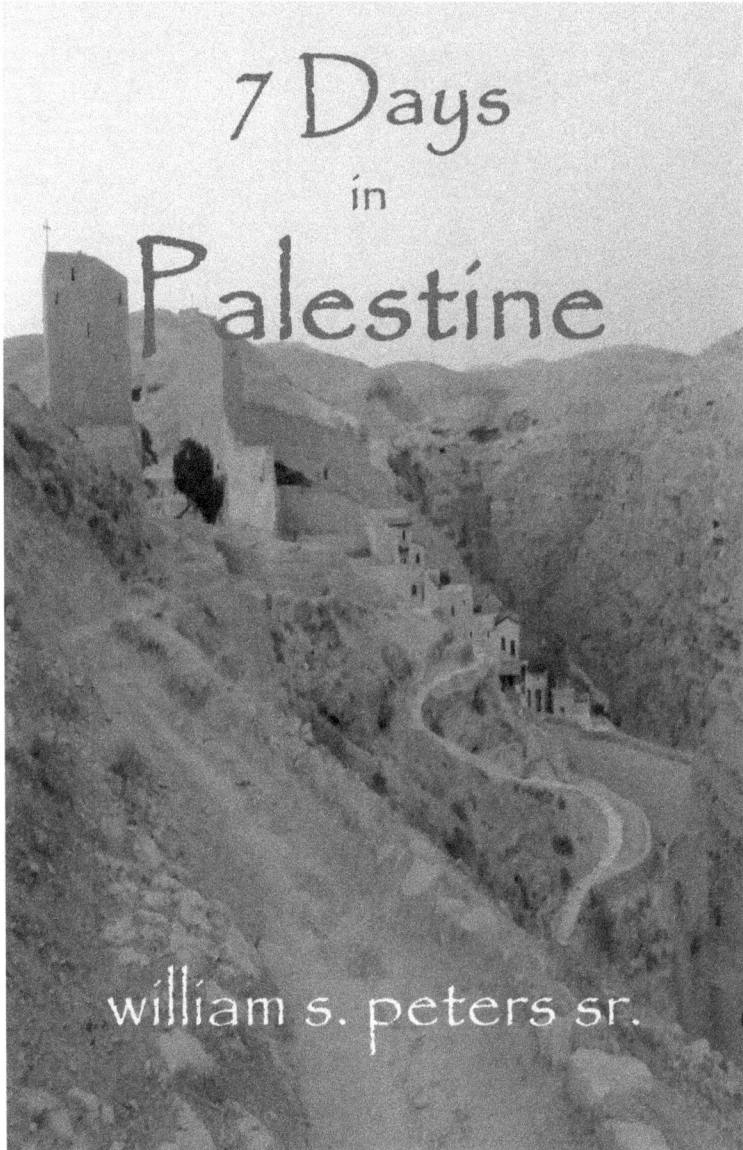

7 Days
in
Palestine

william s. peters sr.

Now Available at
www.innerchildpress.com

inner child press
presents

Tunisia My Love

william s. peters, sr.

Coming in the Summer of 2019

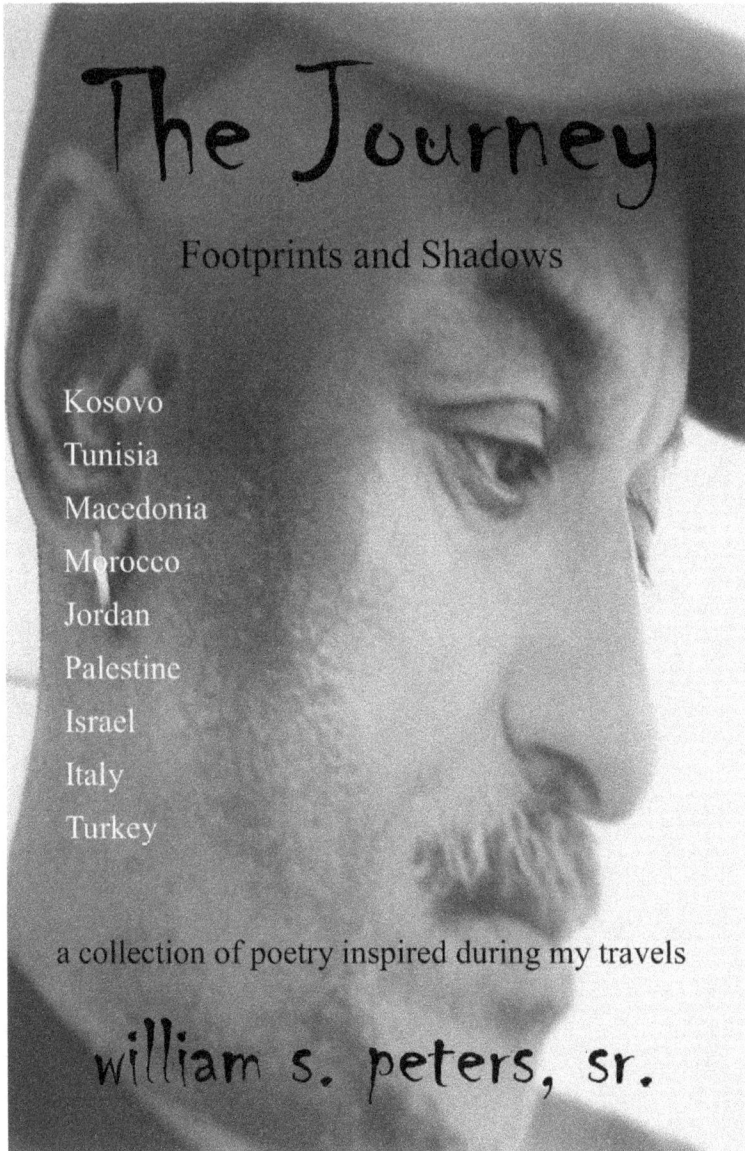

The Journey

Footprints and Shadows

Kosovo

Tunisia

Macedonia

Morocco

Jordan

Palestine

Israel

Italy

Turkey

a collection of poetry inspired during my travels

william s. peters, sr.

Now Available at
www.innerchildpress.com

Now Available at
www.innerchildpress.com

Now Available at
www.innerchildpress.com

Now Available at
www.innerchildpress.com

Inward Reflections

Think on These Things
Book II

william s. peters, sr.

Now Available at
www.innerchildpress.com

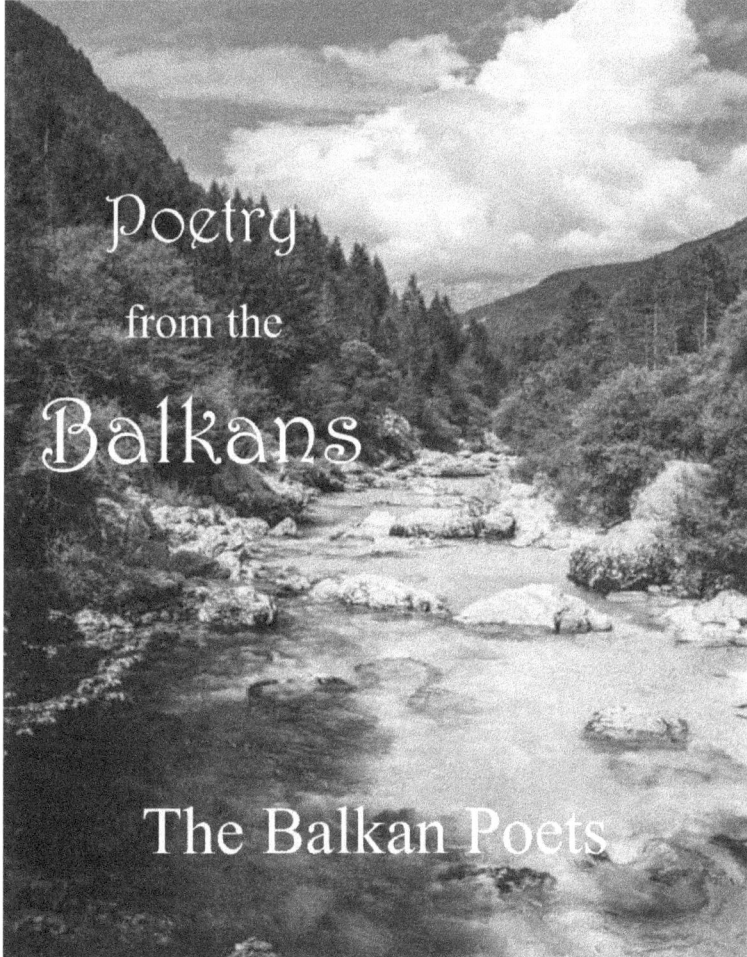

Poetry
from the
Balkans

The Balkan Poets

Other

Anthological

works from

Inner Child Press International

www.innerchildpress.com

Inner Child Press International
presents

A Love Anthology
2019

The Love Poets

Now Available

www.worldhealingworldpeacepoetry.com

Now Available

www.worldhealingworldpeacepoetry.com

Now Available

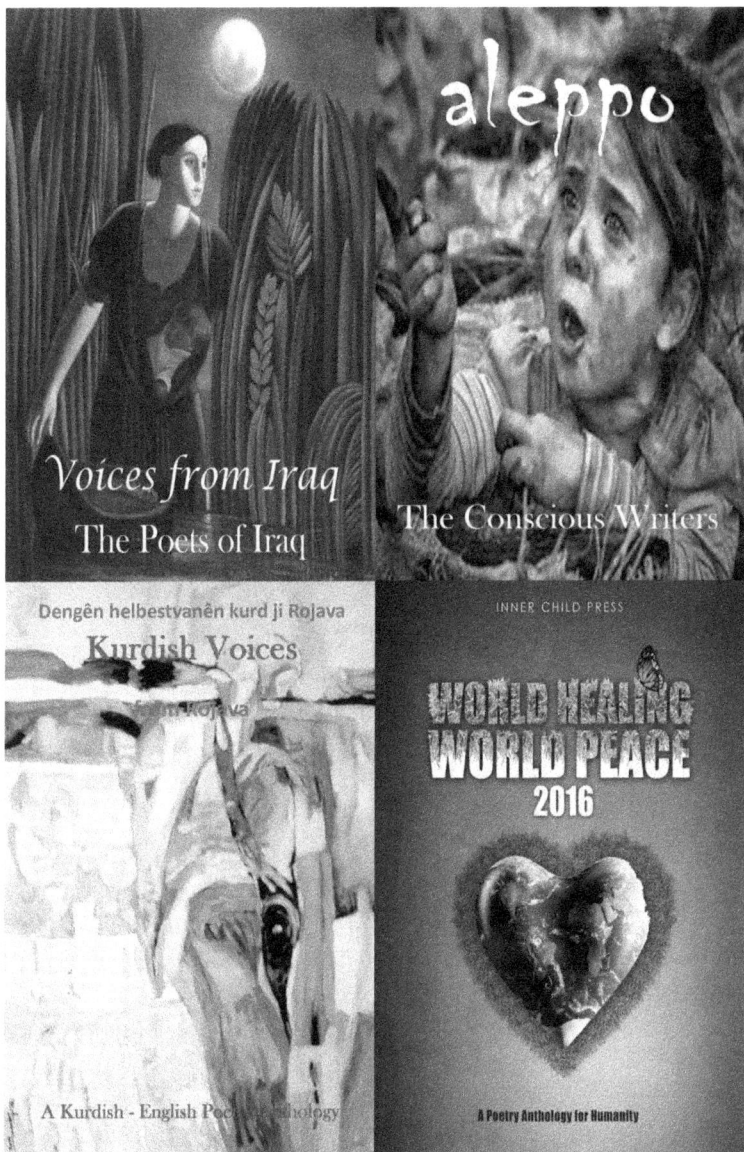

Voices from Iraq
The Poets of Iraq

aleppo
The Conscious Writers

Dengên helbestvanên kurd ji Rojava
Kurdish Voices
A Kurdish - English Poetry Anthology

INNER CHILD PRESS
WORLD HEALING
WORLD PEACE
2016
A Poetry Anthology for Humanity

Now Available

Now Available

www.innerchildpress.com/anthologies

healing through words

Poetry ... Prose ... Prayer ... Stories

a
Poetically
Spoken
Anthology
volume I
Collector's Edition

The Poetry Posse
Presents

an anthology
of

Love

The Poetry Posse 2016

Now Available

www.innerchildpress.com/anthologies

Now Available

www.innerchildpress.com/anthologies

The Year of the Poet
January 2014

The Poetry Posse

Jamie Bond
Gail Weston Shazor
Albert 'Infinite' Carrasco
Siddartha Beth Pierce
Janet P. Caldwell
June 'Bugg' Barefield
Debbie M. Allen
Tony Henninger
Joe DaVerbal Minddancer
Robert Gibbons
Neetu Wali
Shareef Abdur-Rasheed
William S. Peters, Sr.

Carnation

Our January Feature
Terri L. Johnson

the Year of the Poet
February 2014

violets

The Poetry Posse
Jamie Bond
Gail Weston Shazor
Albert 'Infinite' Carrasco
Siddartha Beth Pierce
Janet P. Caldwell
June 'Bugg' Barefield
Debbie M. Allen
Tony Henninger
Joe DaVerbal Minddancer
Robert Gibbons
Neetu Wali
Shareef Abdur-Rasheed
William S. Peters, Sr.

Our February Features
Teresa E. Gallion & Robert Gibson

the Year of the Poet
March 2014

The Poetry Posse
Jamie Bond
Gail Weston Shazor
Albert 'Infinite' Carrasco
Siddartha Beth Pierce
Janet P. Caldwell
June 'Bugg' Barefield
Debbie M. Allen
Tony Henninger
Joe DaVerbal Minddancer
Robert Gibbons
Neetu Wali
Shareef Abdur-Rasheed
Kimberly Burnham
William S. Peters, Sr.

daffodil

Our March Featured Poets
Alicia C. Cooper & hülya yılmaz

the Year of the Poet
April 2014

The Poetry Posse
Jamie Bond
Gail Weston Shazor
Albert 'Infinite' Carrasco
Siddartha Beth Pierce
Janet P. Caldwell
June 'Bugg' Barefield
Debbie M. Allen
Tony Henninger
Joe DaVerbal Minddancer
Robert Gibbons
Neetu Wali
Shareef Abdur-Rasheed
Kimberly Burnham
William S. Peters, Sr.

Our April Featured Poets
Fahredin Shehu
Martina Reisz Newberry
Justin Blackburn
Monte Smith

Sweet Pea

celebrating international poetry month

Now Available

www.innerchildpress.com/the-year-of-the-poet

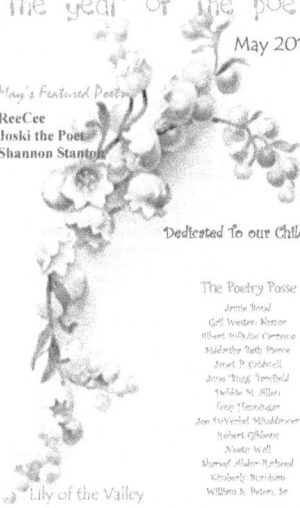

the year of the poet
May 2014

May's Featured Poets
ReeCee
Joski the Poet
Shannon Stanton

Dedicated To our Children

The Poetry Posse

Lily of the Valley

the Year of the Poet
June 2014

Love & Relationship

Rose

June's Featured Poets
Shantelle McLin
Jacqueline D. E. Kennedy
Abraham N. Benjamin

The Poetry Posse

The Year of the Poet
July 2014

July Feature Poets
Christena A. V. Williams
Dr. John R. Strum
Kolade Olanrewaju Freedom

The Poetry Posse

Lotus
Asian Flower of the Month

The Year of the Poet
August 2014

Gladiolus

The Poetry Posse

August Feature Poets
Ann White • Rosalind Cherry • Sheila Jenkins

Now Available

www.innerchildpress.com/the-year-of-the-poet

The Year of the Poet
September 2014

Aster   Morning-Glory

Wild Clematis September Birthday Flower

September Feature Poets
Florence Rulone * Keith Alan Hamilton

The Poetry Posse
Jamie Bond * Gail Weston Shazor * Albert 'Infinite' Carrasco * Siddartha Beth Pierce
Janet P. Caldwell * June 'Bugg' Barefield * Debbie M. Allen * Tony Henninger
Joe DaVerbal Minddancer * Robert Gibbons * Neetu Wali * Shareef Abdur-Rasheed
Kimberly Burnham * William S. Peters, Sr.

THE YEAR OF THE POET
October 2014

Red Poppy

The Poetry Posse
Jamie Bond * Gail Weston Shazor * Albert 'Infinite' Carrasco * Siddartha Beth Pierce
Janet P. Caldwell * June 'Bugg' Barefield * Debbie M. Allen * Tony Henninger
Joe DaVerbal Minddancer * Robert Gibbons * Neetu Wali * Shareef Abdur-Rasheed
Kimberly Burnham * William S. Peters, Sr.

October Feature Poets
Ceri Naz * Rajendra Padhi * Elizabeth Castillo

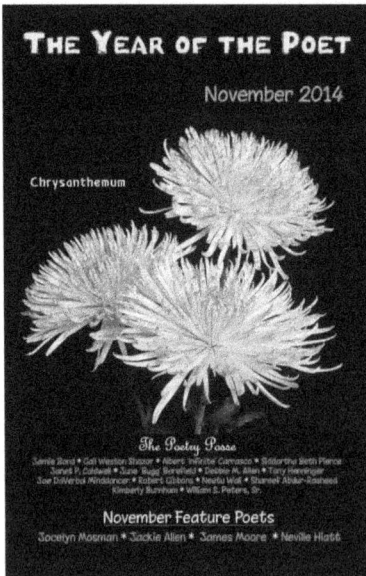

THE YEAR OF THE POET
November 2014

Chrysanthemum

The Poetry Posse
Jamie Bond * Gail Weston Shazor * Albert 'Infinite' Carrasco * Siddartha Beth Pierce
Janet P. Caldwell * June 'Bugg' Barefield * Debbie M. Allen * Tony Henninger
Joe DaVerbal Minddancer * Robert Gibbons * Neetu Wali * Shareef Abdur-Rasheed
Kimberly Burnham * William S. Peters, Sr.

November Feature Poets
Jocelyn Mosman * Jackie Allen * James Moore * Neville Hiatt

The Year of the Poet
December 2014

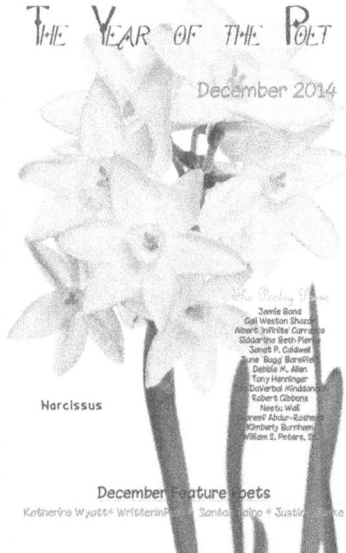

The Poetry Posse
Jamie Bond
Gail Weston Shazor
Albert 'Infinite' Carrasco
Siddartha Beth Pierce
Janet P. Caldwell
June 'Bugg' Barefield
Debbie M. Allen
Tony Henninger
DaVerbal Minddancer
Robert Gibbons
Neetu Wali
Shareef Abdur-Rasheed
Kimberly Burnham
William S. Peters, Sr.

Narcissus

December Feature Poets
Katherine Wyatt* Writtenn... * Santa... lino * Justi... ...e

Now Available

www.innerchildpress.com/the-year-of-the-poet

THE YEAR OF THE POET ii
January 2015

Garnet

The Poetry Posse

Jamie Bond
Gail Weston Shazor
Albert 'Infinite' Carrasco
Siddartha Beth Pierce
Janet P. Caldwell
Tony Henninger
Joe DaVerbal Minddancer
Robert Gibbons
Neetu Wali
Shareef Abdur – Rasheed
Kimberly Burnham
Ann White
Keith Alan Hamilton
Katherine Wyatt
Fahredin Shehu
Hülya N. Yılmaz
Teresa E. Gallion
Jackie Allen
William S. Peters, Sr.

January Feature Poets
Bismay Mohanti * Jen Walls * Eric Judah

THE YEAR OF THE POET ii
February 2015

Amethyst

THE POETRY POSSE

Jamie Bond
Gail Weston Shazor
Albert 'Infinite' Carrasco
Siddartha Beth Pierce
Janet P. Caldwell
Tony Henninger
Joe DaVerbal Minddancer
Robert Gibbons
Neetu Wali
Shareef Abdur – Rasheed
Ann White
Keith Alan Hamilton
Katherine Wyatt
Fahredin Shehu
Hülya N. Yılmaz
Teresa E. Gallion
Jackie Allen
William S. Peters, Sr.

FEBRUARY FEATURE POETS
Iram Fatima * Bob McNeil * Kerstin Centervall

The Year of the Poet II
March 2015

Our Featured Poets
Heung Sook * Anthony Arnold * Alicia Poland

Bloodstone

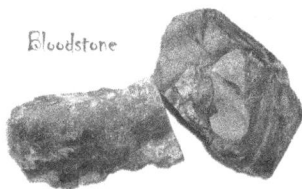

The Poetry Posse 2015
Jamie Bond * Gail Weston Shazor * Albert 'Infinite' Carrasco
Siddartha Beth Pierce * Janet P. Caldwell * Tony Henninger
Joe DaVerbal Minddancer * Neetu Wali * Shareef Abdur – Rasheed
Kimberly Burnham * Ann White * Keith Alan Hamilton
Katherine Wyatt * Fahredin Shehu * Hülya N. Yılmaz
Teresa E. Gallion * Jackie Allen * William S. Peters, Sr

The Year of the Poet II
April 2015

Celebrating International Poetry Month

Our Featured Poets
Raja Williams * Dennis Ferado * Laure Charazac

Diamonds

The Poetry Posse 2015
Jamie Bond * Gail Weston Shazor * Albert 'Infinite' Carrasco
Siddartha Beth Pierce * Janet P. Caldwell * Tony Henninger
Joe DaVerbal Minddancer * Neetu Wali * Shareef Abdur – Rasheed
Kimberly Burnham * Ann White * Keith Alan Hamilton
Katherine Wyatt * Fahredin Shehu * Hülya N. Yılmaz
Teresa E. Gallion * Jackie Allen * William S. Peters, Sr

Now Available

www.innerchildpress.com/the-year-of-the-poet

The Year of the Poet II
May 2015

May's Featured Poets
Geri Algeri
Akin Mosi Chimney
Anna Jakubczak

Emeralds

The Poetry Posse 2015
Jamie Bond * Gail Weston Shazor * Albert 'Infinite' Carrasco
Siddartha Beth Pierce * Janet P. Caldwell * Tony Henninger
Joe DaVerbal Minddancer * Neetu Wali * Shareef Abdur – Rasheed
Kimberly Burnham * Ann White * Keith Alan Hamilton
Katherine Wyatt * Fahredin Shehu * Hülya N. Yılmaz
Teresa E. Gallion * Jackie Allen * William S. Peters. Sr.

The Year of the Poet II
June 2015

June's Featured Poets
Anahit Arustamyan * Yvette D. Murrell * Regina A. Walker

Pearl

The Poetry Posse 2015
Jamie Bond * Gail Weston Shazor * Albert 'Infinite' Carrasco
Siddartha Beth Pierce * Janet P. Caldwell * Tony Henninger
Joe DaVerbal Minddancer * Neetu Wali * Shareef Abdur – Rasheed
Kimberly Burnham * Ann White * Keith Alan Hamilton
Katherine Wyatt * Fahredin Shehu * Hülya N. Yılmaz
Teresa E. Gallion * Jackie Allen * William S. Peters. Sr.

The Year of the Poet II
July 2015

The Featured Poets for July 2015
Abhik Shome * Christina Neal * Robert Neal

Rubies

The Poetry Posse 2015
Jamie Bond * Gail Weston Shazor * Albert 'Infinite' Carrasco
Siddartha Beth Pierce * Janet P. Caldwell * Tony Henninger
Joe DaVerbal Minddancer * Neetu Wali * Shareef Abdur – Rasheed
Kimberly Burnham * Ann White * Keith Alan Hamilton
Katherine Wyatt * Fahredin Shehu * Hülya N. Yılmaz
Teresa E. Gallion * Jackie Allen * William S. Peters. Sr.

The Year of the Poet II
August 2015

Peridot

Featured Poets
Gayle Howell
Ann Chalasz
Christopher Schultz

The Poetry Posse 2015
Jamie Bond * Gail Weston Shazor * Albert 'Infinite' Carrasco
Siddartha Beth Pierce * Janet P. Caldwell * Tony Henninger
Joe DaVerbal Minddancer * Neetu Wali * Shareef Abdur – Rasheed
Kimberly Burnham * Ann White * Keith Alan Hamilton
Katherine Wyatt * Fahredin Shehu * Hülya N. Yılmaz
Teresa E. Gallion * Jackie Allen * William S. Peters. Sr.

Now Available

www.innerchildpress.com/the-year-of-the-poet

The Year of the Poet II
September 2015

Featured Poets

Alfreda Ghee   Lonneice Weeks Badley   Demetrios Trifiatis

Sapphires

The Poetry Posse 2015

Jamie Bond * Gail Weston Shazor * Albert 'Infinite' Carrasco
Siddartha Beth Pierce * Janet P. Caldwell * Tony Henninger
Joe DaVerbal Minddancer * Neetu Wali * Shareef Abdur – Rasheed
Kimberly Burnham * Ann White * Keith Alan Hamilton
Katherine Wyatt * Fahredin Shehu * Hülya N. Yilmaz
Teresa E. Gallion * Jackie Allen * William S. Peters. Sr

The Year of the Poet II
October 2015

Featured Poets

Monte Smith * Laura J. Wolfe * William Washington

Opal

The Poetry Posse 2015

Jamie Bond * Gail Weston Shazor * Albert 'Infinite' Carrasco
Siddartha Beth Pierce * Janet P. Caldwell * Tony Henninger
Joe DaVerbal Minddancer * Neetu Wali * Shareef Abdur – Rasheed
Kimberly Burnham * Ann White * Keith Alan Hamilton
Katherine Wyatt * Fahredin Shehu * Hülya N. Yilmaz
Teresa E. Gallion * Jackie Allen * William S. Peters, Sr.

The Year of the Poet II
November 2015

Featured Poets

Alan W. Jankowski
Bismay Mohanty
James Moore

Topaz

The Poetry Posse 2015

Jamie Bond * Gail Weston Shazor * Albert 'Infinite' Carrasco
Siddartha Beth Pierce * Janet P. Caldwell * Tony Henninger
Joe DaVerbal Minddancer * Neetu Wali * Shareef Abdur – Rasheed
Kimberly Burnham * Ann White * Keith Alan Hamilton
Katherine Wyatt * Fahredin Shehu * Hülya N. Yilmaz
Teresa E. Gallion * Jackie Allen * William S. Peters, Sr.

The Year of the Poet II
December 2015

Featured Poets

Kerione Bryan * Michelle Joan Barulich * Neville Hiatt

Turquoise

The Poetry Posse 2015

Jamie Bond * Gail Weston Shazor * Albert 'Infinite' Carrasco
Siddartha Beth Pierce * Janet P. Caldwell * Tony Henninger
Joe DaVerbal Minddancer * Neetu Wali * Shareef Abdur – Rasheed
Kimberly Burnham * Ann White * Keith Alan Hamilton
Katherine Wyatt * Fahredin Shehu * Hülya N. Yilmaz
Teresa E. Gallion * Jackie Allen * William S. Peters, Sr.

Now Available

www.innerchildpress.com/the-year-of-the-poet

181

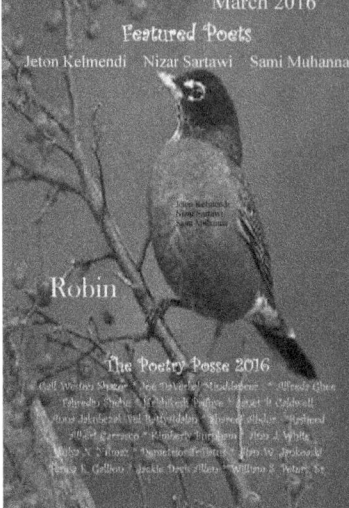

The Year of the Poet III
January 2016

Featured Poets
Lana Joseph * Atom Cyrus Rush * Christena Williams

Dark-eyed Junco

The Poetry Posse 2016

The Year of the Poet III
February 2016

Featured Poets
Anthony Arnold
Anna Chalasz
André Hav...

Puffin

The Poetry Posse 2016

The Year of the Poet
March 2016
Featured Poets
Jeton Kelmendi   Nizar Sartawi   Sami Muhanna

Robin

The Poetry Posse 2016

The Year of the Poet III

Featured Poets

Ali Abdolrezaei

Anna Chalasz

Agim Vinca

Ceri Naz

Black Capped Chickadee

The Poetry Posse 2016

celebrating international poetry month

Now Available

www.innerchildpress.com/the-year-of-the-poet

The Year of the Poet III
May 2016

Bob Strum
Barbara Allan
D.L. Davis

Oriole

The Poetry Posse 2016

The Year of the Poet III
June 2016

Featured Poets

Qibrije Demiri- Frangu
Naime Beqiraj
Faleeha Hassan
Bedri Zyberaj

Black Necked Stilt

The Poetry Posse 2016

The Year of the Poet III
July 2016

Featured Poets

Tram Fatima 'Ashi'
Langley Shazor
Jody Doty
Emilia T. Davis

Indigo Bunting

The Poetry Posse 2016

The Year of the Poet III
August 2016

Featured Poets

Anita Dash
Irena Jovanovic
Malgorzata Gouluda

Painted Bunting

The Poetry Posse 2016

Now Available

www.innerchildpress.com/the-year-of-the-poet

The Year of the Poet III
September 2016

Featured Poets

Simone Weber
Abhijit Sen
Eunice Barbara C. Novio

Long Billed Curle

The Poetry Posse 2016

The Year of the Poet III
October 2016

Featured Poets

Santa Joseph
Ra Krishnamurthy R
Carmen Moun

Barn Owl

The Poetry Posse 2016

The Year of the Poet III
November 2016

Featured Poets

Rosemary Burns
Robin Ouzman Hislop
Lonneice Weeks-Badley

Northern Cardinal

The Poetry Posse 2016

The Year of the Poet III
December 2016

Featured Poets

Samih Masoud
Mountassir Aziz Bien
Abdulkadir Musa

Rough Legged Hawk

The Poetry Posse 2016

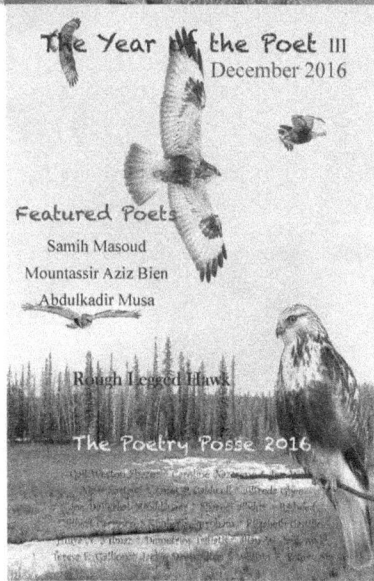

Now Available

www.innerchildpress.com/the-year-of-the-poet

The Year of the Poet IV
January 2017

Featured Poets
Jon Winell
Natalie Shields
Irani Fatima Aslii

Quaking Aspen

The Poetry Posse 2017

The Year of the Poet IV
February 2017

Featured Poets
Lin Ross
Soukaina Fathi
Anwer Ghani

Witch Hazel

The Poetry Posse 2017

The Year of the Poet IV
March 2017

Featured Poets
Tremell Stevens
Francisca Rieinski
Jamil Abu Shaih

The Eastern Redbud

The Poetry Posse 2017

The Year of the Poet IV
April 2017

Featured Poets
Dr. Ruchida Raeniao
Neptune Baroman
Masood Khalaf

The Blossoming Cherry

The Poetry Posse 2017

Now Available

www.innerchildpress.com/the-year-of-the-poet

The Year of the Poet IV
May 2017

The Flowering Dogwood Tree

Featured Poets
Kallisa Powell
Alicja Maria Kuberska
Fethi Sassi

The Poetry Posse 2017

Gail Weston Shazor * Caroline Nazareno * Jhuma Mohanty
Teresa E. Gallion * Anna Jakubczak Vel Ratty Adalan
Joe DaVerbal Minddancer * Shareef Abdur – Rasheed
Albert Carrasco * Kimberly Burnham * Elizabeth Castillo
Hülya N. Yılmaz * Falecha Hassan * Jackie Davis Allen
Jen Walls * Nizar Sartawi * * William S. Peters, Sr

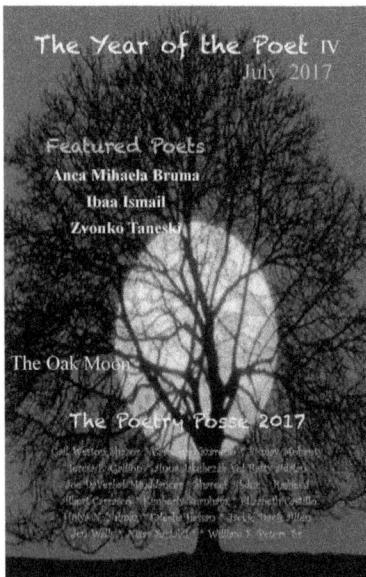

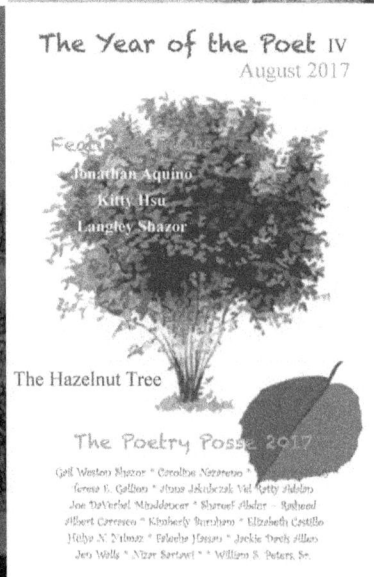

The Year of the Poet IV
June 2017

Featured Poets
Eliza Segiet
Tze-Min Tsai
Abdulla Issa

The Linden Tree

The Poetry Posse 2017

Gail Weston Shazor * Caroline Nazareno * Jhuma Mohanty
Teresa E. Gallion * Anna Jakubczak Vel Ratty Adalan
Joe DaVerbal Minddancer * Shareef Abdur – Rasheed
Albert Carrasco * Kimberly Burnham * Elizabeth Castillo
Hülya N. Yılmaz * Falecha Hassan * Jackie Davis Allen
Jen Walls * Nizar Sartawi * * William S. Peters, Sr

The Year of the Poet IV
July 2017

Featured Poets
Anca Mihaela Bruma
Ibaa Ismail
Zvonko Taneski

The Oak Moon

The Poetry Posse 2017

Gail Weston Shazor * Caroline Nazareno * Jhuma Mohanty
Teresa E. Gallion * Anna Jakubczak Vel Ratty Adalan
Joe DaVerbal Minddancer * Shareef Abdur – Rasheed
Albert Carrasco * Kimberly Burnham * Elizabeth Castillo
Hülya N. Yılmaz * Falecha Hassan * Jackie Davis Allen
Jen Walls * Nizar Sartawi * * William S. Peters, Sr

The Year of the Poet IV
August 2017

Featured Poets
Jonathan Aquino
Kitty Hsu
Langley Shazor

The Hazelnut Tree

The Poetry Posse 2017

Gail Weston Shazor * Caroline Nazareno *
Teresa E. Gallion * Anna Jakubczak Vel Ratty Adalan
Joe DaVerbal Minddancer * Shareef Abdur – Rasheed
Albert Carrasco * Kimberly Burnham * Elizabeth Castillo
Hülya N. Yılmaz * Falecha Hassan * Jackie Davis Allen
Jen Walls * Nizar Sartawi * * William S. Peters, Sr.

Now Available

www.innerchildpress.com/the-year-of-the-poet

The Year of the Poet IV
September 2017

Featured Poets

Martina Reisz Newber

Ameer Nassir

Christine Fulco Neal

Robert Neal

The Elm Tree

The Poetry Posse 2017

Gail Weston Shazor * Caroline Nazareno * Bismay Mohanty
Teresa E. Gallion * Anna Jakubczak Vel Ratty Adalan
Joe DaVerbal Minddancer * Shareef Abdur – Rasheed
Albert Carrasco * Kimberly Burnham * Elizabeth Castillo
Hülya N. Yilmaz * Faleeha Hassan * Jackie Davis Allen
Jen Walls * Nizar Sartawi * * William S. Peters, Sr.

The Year of the Poet IV
October 2017

Featured Poets

Ahmed Abu Saleem

Nedal Al-Qaeim

Sadeddin Shatto

The Black Walnut Tree

The Poetry Posse 2017

Gail Weston Shazor * Caroline Nazareno * Bismay Mohanty
Teresa E. Gallion * Anna Jakubczak Vel Ratty Adalan
Joe DaVerbal Minddancer * Shareef Abdur – Rasheed
Albert Carrasco * Kimberly Burnham * Elizabeth Castillo
Hülya N. Yilmaz * Faleeha Hassan * Jackie Davis Allen
Jen Walls * Nizar Sartawi * * William S. Peters, Sr.

The Year of the Poet IV
November 2017

Featured Poets

Kay Peters

Alfreda D. Ghee

Gabriella Garofalo

Rosemary Cappello

The Tree of Life

The Poetry Posse 2017

Gail Weston Shazor * Caroline Nazareno * Bismay Mohanty
Teresa E. Gallion * Anna Jakubczak Vel Ratty Adalan
Joe DaVerbal Minddancer * Shareef Abdur – Rasheed
Albert Carrasco * Kimberly Burnham * Elizabeth Castillo
Hülya N. Yilmaz * Faleeha Hassan * Jackie Davis Allen
Jen Walls * Nizar Sartawi * William S. Peters, Sr.

The Year of the Poet IV
December 2017

Featured Poets

Justice Clarke

Mariel M. Pabroa

Kiley Brown

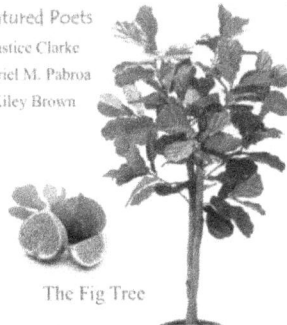

The Fig Tree

The Poetry Posse 2017

Gail Weston Shazor * Caroline Nazareno * Bismay Mohanty
Teresa E. Gallion * Anna Jakubczak Vel Ratty Adalan
Joe DaVerbal Minddancer * Shareef Abdur – Rasheed
Albert Carrasco * Kimberly Burnham * Elizabeth Castillo
Hülya N. Yilmaz * Faleeha Hassan * Jackie Davis Allen
Jen Walls * Nizar Sartawi * William S. Peters, Sr.

Now Available

www.innerchildpress.com/the-year-of-the-poet

The Year of the Poet V
January 2018

Featured Poets

Iyad Shamasnah

Yasmeen Hamzeh

Ali Abdolrezaei

Aksum

The Poetry Posse 2018

Gail Weston Shazor * Caroline Nazareno * Tezmin Ition Tsai
Hülya N. Yılmaz * Faleeha Hassan * Jackie Davis Allen
Teresa E. Gallion * Anna Jakubczak Vel Ratty Adalan
Alicja Maria Kuberska * Shareef Abdur – Rasheed
Kimberly Burnham * Elizabeth Castillo
Nizar Sartawi * William S. Peters, Sr

The Year of the Poet V
February 2018

Sabean

Featured Poets

Muhammad Azram

Anna Szawrucka

Abhilipsa Kuanar

Aanika Aery

The Poetry Posse 2018

Gail Weston Shazor * Caroline Nazareno * Tezmin Ition Tsai
Hülya N. Yılmaz * Faleeha Hassan * Jackie Davis Allen
Teresa E. Gallion * Anna Jakubczak Vel Ratty Adalan
Alicja Maria Kuberska * Shareef Abdur – Rasheed
Kimberly Burnham * Elizabeth Castillo
Nizar Sartawi * William S. Peters, Sr

The Year of the Poet V
March 2018

Featured Poets

Iram Fatima 'Ashi'
Cassandra Sinran
Jaleel Khazual
Shazia Zaman

Mexico   Cuba

Caribbean
&
Middle America

The Poetry Posse 2018

Gail Weston Shazor * Nizar Sartawi * Hülya N. Yılmaz
Jackie Davis Allen * Caroline 'Ceri' Nazareno
Alicja Maria Kuberska * Teresa E. Gallion
Faleeha Hassan * Shareef Abdur – Rasheed
Kimberly Burnham * Elizabeth Castillo
Tezmin Ition Tsai * William S. Peters, Sr.

The Year of the Poet V
April 2018

Featured Poets

The Nez Perce

The Poetry Posse 2018

Now Available

www.innerchildpress.com/the-year-of-the-poet

The Year of the Poet V
May 2018

Featured Poets
Zakry Canción de León Jr.
Sylwia K. Malinowska
Linslita Ahmeti
Ofelia Prodan

The Sumerians

The Poetry Posse 2018

Gail Weston Shazor * Nizar Sartawi * Hülya N. Yılmaz
Jackie Davis Allen * Caroline 'Ceri' Nazareno
Alicja Maria Kuberska * Teresa E. Gallion
Kimberly Burnham * Shareef Abdur – Rasheed
Faleeha Hassan * Elizabeth Castillo * Swapna Behera
Tezmin Ition Tsai * William S. Peters, Sr.

The Year of the Poet V
June 2018

Featured Poets
Isitali Mahiqi * Daim Mißari * Gojko Božović * Sofija Živković

The Paleo Indians

The Poetry Posse 2018

Gail Weston Shazor * Nizar Sartawi * Hülya N. Yılmaz
Jackie Davis Allen * Caroline 'Ceri' Nazareno
Alicja Maria Kuberska * Teresa E. Gallion
Kimberly Burnham * Shareef Abdur – Rasheed
Faleeha Hassan * Elizabeth Castillo * Swapna Behera
Tezmin Ition Tsai * William S. Peters, Sr.

The Year of the Poet V
July 2018

Featured Poets
Padmaja Iyengar-Paddy
Mohammad Ikbal Harb
Eliza Segiet
Tom Higgins

Oceania

The Poetry Posse 2018

Gail Weston Shazor * Nizar Sartawi * Hülya N. Yılmaz
Jackie Davis Allen * Caroline 'Ceri' Nazareno
Alicja Maria Kuberska * Teresa E. Gallion
Kimberly Burnham * Shareef Abdur – Rasheed
Faleeha Hassan * Elizabeth Castillo * Swapna Behera
Tezmin Ition Tsai * William S. Peters, Sr.

The Year of the Poet V
August 2018

Featured Poets
Hussein Habasch * Mircea Dan Duta * Naida Mujkić * Swagat Das

The Lapita

The Poetry Posse 2018

Gail Weston Shazor * Nizar Sartawi * Hülya N. Yılmaz
Jackie Davis Allen * Caroline 'Ceri' Nazareno
Alicja Maria Kuberska * Teresa E. Gallion
Kimberly Burnham * Shareef Abdur – Rasheed
Ashok K. Bhargava* Elizabeth Castillo * Swapna Behaera
Tezmin Ition Tsai * William S. Peters, Sr.

Now Available

www.innerchildpress.com/the-year-of-the-poet

The Year of the Poet V
September 2018

The Aztecs & Incas

Featured Poets
Kolade Olanrewaju Freedom
Iften Scaret
Mazher Hussain Abdul Ghani
Lily Swarn

The Poetry Posse 2018

Gail Weston Shazor * Nizar Sartawi * Hülya N. Yılmaz
Jackie Davis Allen * Caroline 'Ceri' Nazareno
Alicja Maria Kuberska * Teresa E. Gallion
Kimberly Burnham * Shareef Abdur - Rasheed
Ashok K. Bhargava * Elizabeth Castillo * Swapna Behera
Tezmin Ition Tsai * William S. Peters, Sr.

The Year of the Poet V
October 2018

Featured Poets
Alicia Minjarez * Lonnice Weeks-Batley
Lopamudra Mishra * Abdelwahed Souayah

Bengali

The Poetry Posse 2018

Gail Weston Shazor * Nizar Sartawi * Hülya N. Yılmaz
Jackie Davis Allen * Caroline 'Ceri' Nazareno
Alicja Maria Kuberska * Teresa E. Gallion
Kimberly Burnham * Shareef Abdur - Rasheed
Ashok K. Bhargava * Elizabeth Castillo * Swapna Behera
Tezmin Ition Tsai * William S. Peters, Sr.

The Year of the Poet V
November 2018

Featured Poets
Michelle Joan Barnlich * Monsif Beroual
Krystyna Konecka * Nassira Nezzar

The Poetry Posse 2018

Gail Weston Shazor * Nizar Sartawi * Hülya N. Yılmaz
Jackie Davis Allen * Caroline 'Ceri' Nazareno
Alicja Maria Kuberska * Teresa E. Gallion
Kimberly Burnham * Shareef Abdur - Rasheed
Ashok K. Bhargava * Elizabeth Castillo * Swapna Behera
Tezmin Ition Tsai * William S. Peters, Sr.

The Year of the Poet V
December 2018

Featured Poets
Rose Terranova Cirigliano
Joanna Kalinowska
Sokolović Emir
Dr. T. Ashok Chakravarthy

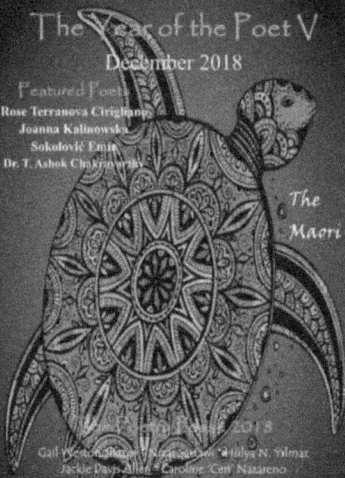

The Maori

The Poetry Posse 2018

Gail Weston Shazor * Nizar Sartawi * Hülya N. Yılmaz
Jackie Davis Allen * Caroline 'Ceri' Nazareno
Alicja Maria Kuberska * Teresa E. Gallion
Kimberly Burnham * Shareef Abdur - Rasheed
Ashok K. Bhargava * Elizabeth Castillo * Swapna Behera
Tezmin Ition Tsai * William S. Peters, Sr.

Now Available

www.innerchildpress.com/the-year-of-the-poet

The Year of the Poet VI
January 2019

Indigenous North Americans

Featured Poets

Houda Elfchtali
Anthony Briscoe
Iram Fatima 'Ashi'
Dr. K. K. Mathew

Dream Catcher

The Poetry Posse 2019

Gail Weston Shazor * Joe Paire * Hülya N. Yılmaz
Jackie Davis Allen * Caroline Nazareno * Eliza Segiet
Alicja Maria Kuberska * Teresa E. Gallion
Kimberly Burnham * Shareef Abdur – Rasheed
Ashok K. Bhargava * Elizabeth Castillo * Swapna Behera
Tezmin Ition Tsai * William S. Peters, Sr.

The Year of the Poet VI
February 2019

Featured Poets

Marek Lukaszewicz * Bharati Nayak
Aida G. Roque * Jean-Jacques Fournier

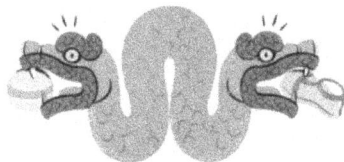

Meso-America

The Poetry Posse 2019

Gail Weston Shazor * Albert Carrasco * Hülya N. Yılmaz
Jackie Davis Allen * Caroline Nazareno * Eliza Segiet
Alicja Maria Kuberska * Teresa E. Gallion * Joe Paire
Kimberly Burnham * Shareef Abdur – Rasheed
Ashok K. Bhargava * Elizabeth Castillo * Swapna Behera
Tezmin Ition Tsai * William S. Peters, Sr.

The Year of the Poet VI
March 2019

Featured Poets

Enesa Mahmić * Sylvia K. Malinowska
Shurouk Hammoud * Anwer Ghani

The Caribbean

Gail Weston Shazor * Albert Carrasco * Hülya N. Yılmaz
Jackie Davis Allen * Caroline Nazareno * Eliza Segiet
Alicja Maria Kuberska * Teresa E. Gallion * Joe Paire
Kimberly Burnham * Shareef Abdur – Rasheed
Ashok K. Bhargava * Elizabeth Castillo * Swapna Behera
Tezmin Ition Tsai * William S. Peters, Sr.

The Year of the Poet VI
April 2019

Featured Poets

DL Davis * Michelle Joan Barulich
Lulëzim Haziri * Faleeha Hassan

Central & West Africa

The Poetry Posse 2019

Gail Weston Shazor * Albert Carrasco * Hülya N. Yılmaz
Jackie Davis Allen * Caroline Nazareno * Eliza Segiet
Alicja Maria Kuberska * Teresa E. Gallion * Joe Paire
Kimberly Burnham * Shareef Abdur – Rasheed
Ashok K. Bhargava * Elizabeth Castillo * Swapna Behera
Tezmin Ition Tsai * William S. Peters, Sr.

Now Available

www.innerchildpress.com/the-year-of-the-poet

The Year of the Poet VI
May 2019

Featured Poets

Emad Al-Haydary * Hussein Nasser Jabr
Wahab Sheriff * Abdul Razzaq Al Ameeri

Asia Southeast Asia and Maritime Asia

The Poetry Posse 2019

Gail Weston Shazor * Albert Carrasco * Hülya N. Yılmaz
Jackie Davis Allen * Caroline Nazareno * Eliza Segiet
Alicja Maria Kuberska * Teresa E. Gallion * Joe Paire
Kimberly Burnham * Shareef Abdur – Rasheed
Ashok K. Bhargava * Elizabeth Castillo * Swapna Behera
Teemin Ition Tsai * William S. Peters, Sr.

The Year of the Poet VI
June 2019

Featured Poets

Kate Gaudi Powiekszone * Sahaj Sabharwai
Iwu Jeff * Mohamed Abdel Aziz Shmeis

Arctic
Circumpolar

The Poetry Posse 2019

Gail Weston Shazor * Albert Carrasco * Hülya N. Yılmaz
Jackie Davis Allen * Caroline Nazareno * Eliza Segiet
Alicja Maria Kuberska * Teresa E. Gallion * Joe Paire
Kimberly Burnham * Shareef Abdur – Rasheed
Ashok K. Bhargava * Elizabeth Castillo * Swapna Behera
Teemin Ition Tsai * William S. Peters, Sr.

Now Available

www.innerchildpress.com/the-year-of-the-poet

and there is much, much more !

visit . . .

www.innerchildpress.com/antho logies-sales-special.php

Also check out our Authors and all the wonderful Books Available at :

www.innerchildpress.com/autho rs-pages

INNER CHILD PRESS

WORLD HEALING WORLD PEACE
2018

A Poetry Anthology for Humanity

Now Available

www.worldhealingworldpeacepoetry.com

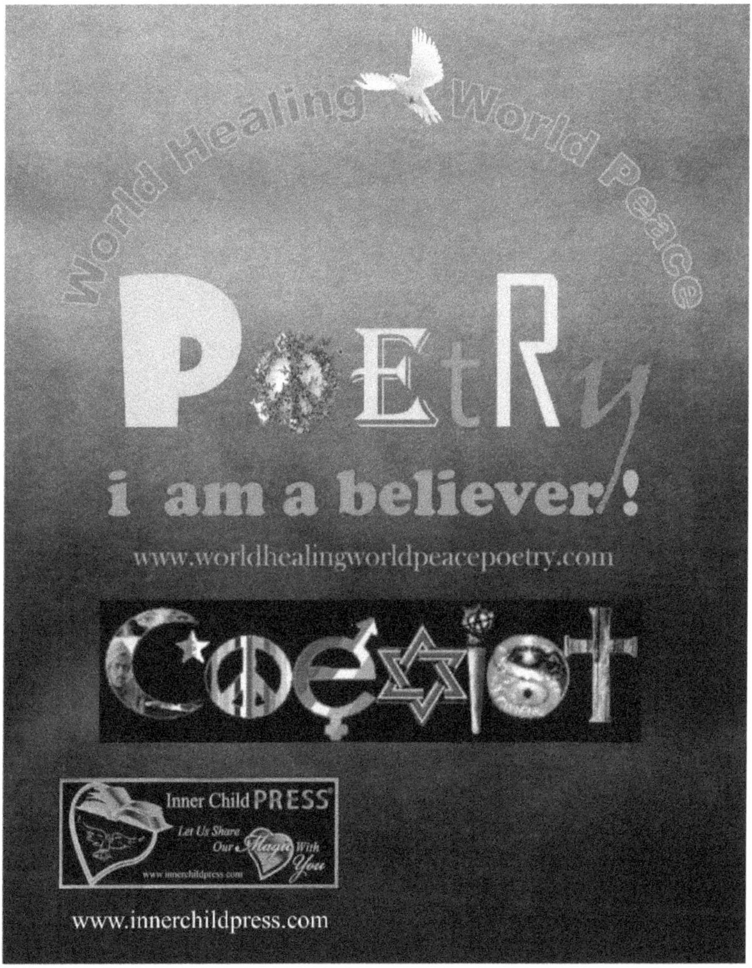

Now Available

www.worldhealingworldpeacepoetry.com

i support

World Healing
World Peace

www.worldhealingworldpeacepoetry.com

World Healing
World Peace
2018

Now Available

www.worldhealingworldpeacepoetry.com

Inner Child Press International

'building bridges of cultural understanding'

Meet our Cultural Ambassadors

Fahredin Shehu
Director of Cultural

Faleha Hassan
Iraq - USA

Elizabeth E. Castillo
Philippines

Antoinette Coleman
Chicago
Midwest USA

Ananda Nepali
Nepal - East
Southern India

Kimberly Burnham
North Eastern
USA

Alicja Kuberska
Poland
Eastern Europe

Swapna Behera
India
Southeast Asia

Kolade O. Freedom
Nigeria
West Africa

Monsif Beroual
Morocco
Northern Asia

Ashok K. Bhargava
Canada

Tzemin Ition Tsai
Republic of China
Greater China

Alicia M. Ramírez
Mexico
Central America

Christena AV Williams
Jamaica
Caribbean

Louise Rudou
Eastern Canada

Aziz Mountassir
Southern Africa

Shareef Abdur-Rasheed
Southeastern USA

Laure Charazac
France
Western Europe

Mohammud Ikbal Harb
Lebanon
Middle East

Mohamed Abdel
Aziz Shmeis
Egypt
Middle East

Hilary Mainga
Africa
Eastern Africa

Josephus R. Johnson
Liberia

www.innerchildpress.com

This Anthological Publication
is underwritten solely by

Inner Child Press

Inner Child Press is a Publishing Company Founded and Operated by Writers. Our personal publishing experiences provides us an intimate understanding of the sometimes daunting challenges Writers, New and Seasoned may face in the Business of Publishing and Marketing their Creative "Written Work".

For more Information

Inner Child Press

www.innerchildpress.com

Inner Child Press International

'building bridges of cultural understanding'

202 Wiltree Court, State College, Pennsylvania 16801

www.innerchildpress.com

~ fini ~

Coming
April 2020

Inner Child Press International

The
World Healing, World Peace
International Poetry Symposium

Stay Tuned

for more information

intouch@innerchildpress.com

'building bridges of cultural understanding'

www.innerchildpress.com

www.ingramcontent.com/pod-product-compliance
Lightning Source LLC
LaVergne TN
LVHW011154080426
835508LV00007B/391